Illustrators Unlimited

THE ESSENCE Unlimited
OF CONTEMPORARY ILLUSTRATION

gestalten

Introduction

"One thing illustration has always lacked is a strong critical framework by which to assess it," the design critic Rick Poynor wrote in an essay last year, and, as usual, he's right. Precious little material exists when you look for an informed analysis on the state of contemporary illustration, or for that matter, illustration from any historical period. However, given the explosion of quality work during the past decade, perhaps this isn't an altogether negative thing, and it's worth asking which group of people this supposed framework would benefit more: the illustrator, or the critic?

One thing is certain: the lack of a critical framework hasn't hindered the growth of the medium, and you would be tempted to argue that illustrators are perhaps better off because of it— if today's illustrators lack regular, informed evaluation of their progress, they also lack the existential complex that afflicts so many of their graphic design brethren, who seem to be forever agonizing over whether their work is design or whether it is art. Contemporary illustrators appear to betray no fears about the "death of illustration." There are thankfully few books asking, "What is illustration?" Likewise, angst-ridden, best-selling tracts about selling out—or worse, utopian urging for doing good or outsized, oversized tomes about changing the world—are the exception rather than the rule. The aims of illustration are more modest, and perhaps its practitioners are freer for it. Many contemporary illustrators do not even consider themselves illustrators in the traditional sense—illustration is simply something that they do.

It is in this spirit that we introduce Illustrators Unlimited, a book about contemporary illustration. In one sense, it is a picture book, which we hope will inspire those who practice illustration as well as those who aspire to it in either personal or professional situations. And as the title suggests, the book illustrates just how few boundaries exist: there is no set style, no set way. But in another sense, the book is a helpful look at the manner in which contemporary illustrators do their work, how they make their images, the situations in which they discovered their love of drawing, and the interplay between handmade and digital techniques, and the influence that each method has on the other.

Like photography paved the way for painting to become something else—i.e., not representational—so digitalization, animation, and easy manipulation have created an environment for illustration to become simultaneously more decorative and purposeful. One image no longer needs to carry the bulk of the narrative weight, as illustrators have begun supplementing traditional techniques with new ones—silkscreen with layers and layers of Photoshop. It's a hybrid process that can just as easily integrate printmaking's limited color palette with digital reams of patterned textures, scanned bits of sketches filled in with swaths of RGB, or Corel Painter on top of watercolor—a part digital, and part handmade hybrid method that allows for maximum flexibility.

This approach is distinct from the remix, which relies heavily on a primary, recognizable source, and from collage, which is often more piecemeal and abstract. These images will often evoke an overall vintage "type"—art nouveau, 1960s French New Wave, film noir, color by number, pulp comics, erotic novels, My Little Pony—but the process also makes it possible to easily reference the past in a more individualized way. The ability to build up an image with different textures, layer upon layer upon layer, has fundamentally altered the working process.

The work in Illustrators Unlimited fits at various points along this hybrid handmade digital continuum. But even those who fall on the "more handmade" end of the continuum describe their image-making process in similar terms: if it isn't working, cover it up and try something else, keep moving, keep doing, mix and match, and if that doesn't work, add some more, cover, and layer. This is the way artists have always worked; it's just that the tools have expanded. There is even a subtle shift in the way that illustrators describe their work, sometimes describing their craft as "building an image," as if it were a house or a sculpture.

While the obsessive, repetition-based handmade aesthetic that ascended during the 2000s was a necessary corrective to the "slick," computerized illustration of the 1990s, the handmade look is adapting and evolving as well in order to retain its competitive advantage. Finding the right combination of the two allows illustrators to build an image layer by layer while retaining a distinctly human feel, in which the layers are not proscribed, but carefully and meticulously arranged.

This book is not then a catalog of the most experimental illustrators working in this hybrid way. Rather, they have a strong relationship to classical handmade illustration, whether it's executed digitally or not. And in the end, what separates the good from the bad remains the same as always: their craftsmanship, and their skill. The possibilities afforded by Photoshop are simply a normal part of the work these days.

In addition to stylistic influences, they also exhibit a sensibility informted by graphic design, incorporating aspects of composition, perspective, patterning, and scale. Many were formally trained as designers, but consider themselves self-taught as illustrators. And as the visual syntax of certain periods (Edo period Japanese medical illustration, 1950s education pamphlets, 1920s advertisements) or certain artists (the Sternberg Brothers, Henri Matisse, John James Audubon) are mixed in, illustrators refer to their own work beyond the drawn execution. So it makes sense that the illustrators featured here, by and large, are media agnostic. If you want to find a common theme, you could say that they are almost unilaterally pragmatic. It's just whatever gets the job done, resembling nothing so much a theory or a framework as it is a way of working, a way to make, create, and do.

The book is itself a hybrid: it is partly a showcase of the best and most well-known contemporary illustrators, it's also partly a look at lesser-known talents who are worth checking out. Perhaps it's just a coincidence, but there's one other common theme that runs through the book: Many of the illustrators featured here happened to grow up in rural, non-urban environments, from villages in Lapland to the forests of the Pacific Northwest, from suburban sprawl in Israel to the Appalachian Mountains. And the intensive, repetitive layering of much of the work speaks to a style born out of boredom and intuition, each one unique and clear, bounded only by one's own capacity for imagination, a page without limits.

Anna Emilia Laitinen: Apple Blossom Meadow, 2010, Personal

Anna Emilia Laitinen

Anna Emilia Laitinen was born in Leppävirta, a small town in Finland surrounded by strawberry fields, lakes, and pine forests. It was there that she built huts out of branches, listened to stories, and began drawing and painting using thistle flowers for paint brushes. The Finnish weather inspires her color palette, and she enjoys finding connections between nature, and the ones living in it, collecting them as memories on a soft cotton paper. Her watercolors and drawings have been used in magazines and books, and by cultural institutions.

1. **Tea for Five, 2011**
   Kinfolk Magazine
   EDITORIAL * WATERCOLOR

2. **In Feather Islands, 2010**
   Kotiliesi Magazine
   EDITORIAL * WATERCOLOR

3. **Balance, 2011**
   Kaksplus Magazine
   EDITORIAL * WATERCOLOR

4. **Hair Storm, 2011**
   Kaksplus Magazine
   EDITORIAL * WATERCOLOR

5. **Dreaming, 2010**
   The Finnish Association for Persons with Intellectual Disabilities
   POSTER * WATERCOLOR

Oliver Jeffers

Oliver Jeffers has three primary outlets for his work: commercial illustration, painting, and the one that he's most known for, picture book illustration. His book UP AND DOWN was shortlisted for a Children's Book Ireland award this year, while THE HEART AND THE BOTTLE was given the British Book Design Award last year. He is also the author of THE GREAT PAPER CAPER, THE WAY BACK HOME, INCREDIBLE BOOK EATING BOY, LOST AND FOUND, and HOW TO CATCH A STAR. He currently works from a charming studio in Brooklyn, New York.

WHEN DID YOU START DRAWING? I think it was Picasso who said that every child is an artist, the trick is to remain one when you grow up, and I suppose I never really stopped. Once I realized that it was possible to do this as a career, I never looked back. I've always been torn between different types of art that I want to make, and I figured I'll just pursue whichever ones I want to do until I reach some sort of crossroads, or I'm forced to stop one, and I guess I never was forced to choose between them. So I do lots of different sorts of things.

SO YOU DON'T SELF-IDENTIFY AS AN ILLUSTRATOR? Not really, no. But I don't self-identify as a painter either. I don't really know what the hell to call myself, generally, so I usually don't. The boundaries between disciplines are blurring constantly, and it's possible for people now to do more than one artistic practice. It's a hindrance for some but a real asset for others, and it's an environment that I can really thrive in because each aspect of what I do supports the other aspects, and keeps it all afloat. It works for me, at least mentally.

WHAT WERE THE FIRST THINGS YOU STARTED DRAWING? I used to draw massive tidal waves and giant whales. I remember reading the book THE BAD-TEMPERED LADYBIRD, by the writer Eric Carle, where this ladybug picks a fight with different animals of increasing sizes, and at the end picks a fight with a whale. And I remember wondering how did the whale look so enormous when it was in a book that was the same size as all the other animals? Then I realized that it was compared to the ladybug—and it was like letting out a magician's secret, scale, and contrast of scale. So I'd draw a wave and make it a giant wave by putting a tiny boat in it. I'd draw a normal-sized person, but then make them a giant person by putting a tiny house under their foot. Apparently, I was fascinated with carnage.

AND THAT'S A TECHNIQUE THAT YOU STILL EMPLOY TODAY? Definitely, it's a big part of my work—a big empty space can make something look small—and it's a powerful storytelling device when used properly.

WOULD YOU CONSIDER YOURSELF SELF-TAUGHT? In terms of technique, absolutely. I used to sit in on some of the life drawing classes on the fine art side, but a lot of techniques that I use are self-taught. And I have no formal training in painting whatsoever. I've learned just by reading books. How do you clean a brush? I'll look it up in a book. How do you prime a canvas? I'll look it up in a book. How do you make this look like that? Often, I will learn just by looking at the artist's work. How did John Singer Sargent make an ear look like that? He's only done it, like, with three strokes. And I'll look, and dissect it and create it, and then eventually it'll turn into my own way of doing it. It's a lot about preparation and being ready to go, so that when you put brush to canvas or pen to paper, you're prepared so that the spontaneity can happen without any unnecessary obstacles.

BUT YOU DID GO TO ART SCHOOL? Yeah, the degree was actually called visual communication and there was an emphasis on illustration, typography, and advertising. It was method more than technique. But that's absolutely where I understand the basic concepts in layout, and my interest in typography was born there.

1.___**The America Map, 2008**
WIRED Magazine/
You and Me The Royal We
EDITORIAL | HOUSE PAINT | CHALK ON WOOD

2.___**The Incredible Book Eating Boy, 2007**
Personal
CHILDREN BOOK * COLLAGE | PAINT

CAN YOU DESCRIBE THE PROCESS THAT YOU GO THROUGH WHEN MAKING AN IMAGE? Everything starts with a drawing. For my painting, a lot of what happens on the canvas happens there for the first time. I trust my gut a lot more with my painting. For an illustration, it will start with a drawing and then pretty quickly I'll decide on which method of execution I'll choose—watercolor, gouache, collage, digital. The sketches often will not be very detailed because I like for a lot of it to happen on the actual piece. My last book was entirely digital, but out of necessity because of my studio setup at the time. So I would make a bunch of little scribbles and drawings, and paint dribbles on an actual page, and use my tiny scanner, scan them in, and apply the color and layer them up, and would eventually construct the illustration in Photoshop. If I'm doing something in watercolor, I'll do a very detailed line art drawing first, so I know where the text will go or where I need to leave space, where it shouldn't get too dark, things like that.

AND WATERCOLOR CAN BE DIFFICULT TO MANAGE. Yes, often something will happen that I don't want and it'll get scrapped.

IS THAT SPONTANEITY SOMETHING THAT YOU ARE AIMING FOR BY USING THAT MEDIUM? Well, I use watercolors much more like acrylics. I use them really thick and heavy and wait for them to dry before putting something next to them, so there's very little bleeding. And while bleeding does occur, it's deliberate. But there is a spontaneous element for sure.

SO YOUR PROCESS IS PRETTY SIMILAR NO MATTER WHAT MEDIUM YOU'RE USING? Yeah, just layering it up bit by bit by bit. And judging, adjusting, judging, adjusting.

WHAT WOULD YOU SAY IS YOUR FAVORITE THING TO DRAW? There are certain things I will avoid drawing—more nebulous things like sunsets, or painterly-type things—but I like drawing props a lot, random pieces of equipment: I'll furnish a desk in the background with a lamp for no other reason than I enjoy doing it. One illustration was of a girl with her heart in a bottle and there were all these techniques to get her heart out of the bottle: a two-handled ax, a drill, a stick of dynamite, a vacuum cleaner. It's one of my favorites.

NUT BIOLOGY

WALNUT
Lungs

PEANUT
Brain

PINE
Nuts

3. **Nut Biology, 2011**
Personal
PENCIL

4. **Five Hour Map;
Mexico City, 2009**
United Airlines
EDITORIAL*MIXED MEDIA

5. **Japan Politics, 2009**
Newsweek
EDITORIAL*ACRYLIC|COLLAGE|INK

Diana Sudyka

Illustrator and printmaker Diana Sudyka lives and works in Chicago, USA.

Her printmaking background includes working as master printer for studios such as Big Cat Press in Chicago, and Landfall Press, now located in Santa Fe, New Mexico. Currently she creates illustrations for books, albums, and her natural history blog, The Tiny Aviary, which documents her experience volunteering for the Chicago Field Museum of Natural History. She has also created posters for bands such as The Decemberists, Feist, Iron and Wine, Andrew Bird, Modest Mouse, Pearl Jam, and Tortoise. Her recently illustrated books include The Mysterious Benedict Society and the Perilous Journey, and the upcoming The Mysterious Benedict Society and the Prisoner's Dilemma.

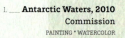
Musk deer

Brecht Evens

Brecht Evens is a cartoonist and illustrator living in Brussels, Belgium. There he creates colorful watercolors for comic books and graphics novels, including his prize-winning, debut comic book, A MESSAGE FROM SPACE (2005) and VINCENT (2006). THE WRONG PLACE, released in 2009, went on to win the Haarlem Comic Festival's Willy Vandersteen Award for best Dutch-language graphic novel. His deluxe comic book NIGHT ANIMALS was published by Top Shelf in 2011. He takes visual inspiration from painters and writers, including David Hockney, Saul Steinberg, medieval/Eastern drawings, and his current read, Albert Cohen's BELLE DU SEIGNEUR.

Anne Smith

Before becoming an illustrator, Anne Smith spent many years working as a potter. Some interests and influences from that earlier time still touch her work such as Staffordshire pottery, Russian revolutionary porcelain, Shaker gift drawings, Alfred Wallis, Ravillious + Bawden, natural history illustration, decorative arts archive pages, typography, and Mugal miniatures. Her editorial, publishing, design, and advertising clients include Starbucks Coffee Co., THE OPRAH MAGAZINE, Simon and Schuster, AUDUBON magazine, and THE GUARDIAN.

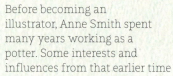

72

22

24

21

A

29

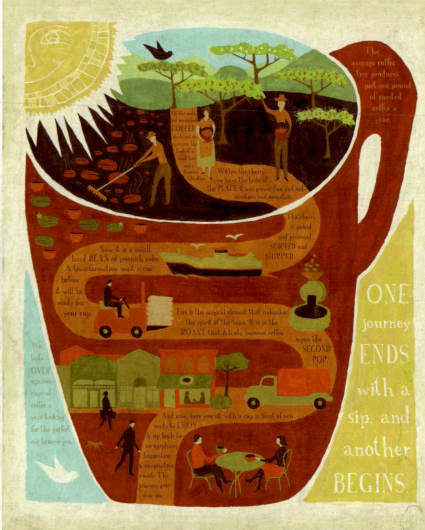

Traci Daberko

1_____ **Whale Promotion, 2011**
Personal
PROMO * PAINTING|DIGITAL

2_____ **Starbucks**
Bean to Cup, 2007
Starbucks
ART DIRECTION: KARI STRAND
POSTER * PAINTING|DIGITAL

3_____ **Starbucks' Tree /**
Mission Statement, 2007
Starbucks
ART DIRECTION BY KARI STRAND
POSTER * PAINTING|DIGITAL

4_____ **Rail-volution, 2010**
Rail-volution
ART DIRECTION: LAURIE CAUSGROVE
BROCHURE * PAINTING|DIGITAL

5_____ **Starbucks Barista**
Dedication, 2007
Starbucks
ART DIRECTION: KARI STRAND
POSTER * DIGITAL

When Traci Daberko started her career as a graphic designer, she found herself exploring the world of illustration. She now thrives on creating inventive imagery using a range of styles such as clean vector lines and shapes, and a detailed approach with painterly colors and textures. Her work has been used for a wide range of clients in annual reports, advertising, product labels, as well as music, entertainment, and fashion illustration. She operates her studio, DBRKO, from Seattle, USA.

There's a dad and daughter who come in every day. They're more than just father and daughter. They're friends.

We have a group that comes in each morning — three generations of about 20 people sitting around tables.

For weeks, I called a customer by the wrong name. He was too shy to correct me. I was so embarrassed when I found out.

Lots of moms come with strollers to our store. It's the baby brigade!

There was a blind date here the other day. The guy walks in red-faced, breaking a sweat, and says, Are you so-and-so?

Sometimes they have a disagreement about who's going to pay for the drinks. "I'm going to get it!" "No, I'm going to get it."

Last Christmas, she baked us the most amazing cookies. It's nice when customers are nice.

He's a man of habit, orders the same thing for breakfast every day. I suggest a new sandwich, he gets that one every day thereafter.

I like to play backgammon with Sam on my breaks, even though he cleans my clock.

Behind every good cup of coffee there is a barista and a good story.

I think Abby has been working on her novel for six years now.

I can identify my regular drive-thru customers by the sounds of their car engines.

I love doing coffee tastings, especially when I can name them blind.

I'm the person who introduced Mary to Iced Vanilla Chai, and now she drinks it every day.

Neil is my human VCR. He's always able to tell me what I missed on TV last night.

There's a mom and the cutest two-year-old who come in for hot chocolate milk, only she calls it dot dot milk.

A customer greeted his wife with flowers and a mocha. It was really sweet.

There's a lovely couple who come in every morning, and read the newspaper to each other.

I have a customer who orders a Triple-Tall Nonfat Extra Hot Cappuccino every day. We call it an Angela.

On game days, people just flood in, wearing school colors and ready to root for their team.

Tracy Walker

Tracy Walker worked for several years as a designer in the book publishing industry before making the leap into a fulltime illustration career. Drawn to the geometry, design, and chaos in the natural forms around her, she uses these shapes in the imagery to communicate her ideas. Walker's work has been recognized by AMERICAN ILLUSTRATION, 3x3 magazine, and the Illustrators Club of Washington DC. and has appeared in newspapers, magazines worldwide, advertising, package design, and children's books worldwide.

Sanna Mander

Finnish illustrator Sanna Mander's work is colorful and highly saturated, and inspired by garden parties and delightful disarray. After studying graphic design at the University of Art and Design Helsinki, her work has begun to go beyond printed media into interiors, tableware, and textiles. As an illustrator and graphic designer, she has won awards such as Cannes Young Creatives 2006 and Junior of the Year 2007 at the Finnish Best of the Year competition. Her recent work includes illustrations for CASAMICA magazine, Marimekko, and Ricky-Tick Records, a poster for the 2011 Pori Jazz Festival, and book covers for the Australian publisher Scribe Publications.

WHEN DID YOU FIRST START TO DRAW? When I was two, my family moved to Stockholm in Sweden, to a typical, concrete suburb with graffiti, tower blocks, and hip-hop music. It was there that I began to draw letters for graffiti pieces with the cool kids while secretly designing friendship booklets with my nerdy pen pals where we would bind our own books, and draw our own cover illustrations with handwritten typography.

SO WOULD YOU SAY YOU ARE LARGELY SELF-TAUGHT? OR HOW DID YOU LEARN? I think I learned to draw just by being a besserwisser [the German equivalent of a "know-it-all"] and always trying to be smarter than the other kids. I must have been around seven when I tried to convince my classmates to mix the colors, not only to use them straight from the color tubes.

DID YOU SHOW UP AT SCHOOL WITH YOUR STYLE AND TECHNIQUE ALREADY DEVELOPED? OR HOW MUCH DID YOUR SCHOOLING AFFECT THE EVOLUTION OF YOUR STYLE? It was really refreshing to go to art school in Helsinki from Stockholm, where it seemed like everyone was following the same contemporary trends. I was born in Lapland, in the northern part of Finland—we had reindeer walking around in the backyard, and I remember wearing red felt boots in the snow. Helsinki was totally off the map in that sense. Everybody was just doing their thing, and nobody seemed to care if their work was hip or not. I felt very shallow, so I spent a couple of years trying all these different styles and techniques, and finding my thing. But it wasn't until years after school I quit trying to be cool and began to draw like I wanted!

WHO WOULD YOU SAY WAS AN EARLY INSPIRATION FOR YOU? As a kid, I lived two floors up from the library, so I spent a lot of time there, studying children's books and reading comics. Like many other melancholic Finnish people, there is something about Tove Jansson's illustrations that fascinates me. The characters are untypical: charming, but not too sweet, like how there is salt in Finnish chocolate. The images can be graphic and punchy, but they can detailed and sensitive, too.

WERE THERE ANY INTERNATIONAL INFLUENCES AS WELL? My mother was a typical working class single mother, and I didn't have many books nor toys. But the ones I had were all Happy Meal toys or Disney crap—pastel-colored and mass-produced. Maybe that's why I'm into the aesthetics of the 1950s and '60s, where there's a consideration for quality and thought. And as a teenager, I read independent comics a lot; when I saw Chris Ware's comics for the first time, everything changed.

HOW DO YOU BEGIN WHEN YOU SIT DOWN TO CREATE AN IMAGE? Visualizing things has always been easy for me. Normally when I get a brief moment, I instantly start getting ideas for the final work. Sometimes I see the end result as drawn by someone else, perhaps someone who would be better for the job. I usually don't need to sketch something on paper to find an idea. It can be a shape, or even a mistake that solves it. I draw the basic shapes in Freehand, then continue with them in Photoshop, often adding in some drawing with the Wacom pen, and then finally I add different scanned textures, and adjust far too many layers for far too long.

SO IT'S A COMBINATION OF HAND-DRAWN AND DIGITAL ELEMENTS? I draw a lot by hand for myself, but nowadays I don't have the patience to build up hand-drawn images for clients the same way I do in Photoshop. Yet, I think my drawn lines are better handdrawn, so I will do something with that in the future. But as all scanners are ugly, I refuse to buy one.

WHAT IS YOUR ALL-TIME FAVORITE THING TO DRAW? I never get tired of drawing flowers or girls. Food is great as well, and organic shapes and colors in endless variations. I often buy flower bouquets, and the ones I can't buy I'm very happy to be able to draw!

Sami Viljanto

Finish illustrator Sami Viljanto's colorful digital images can be found in editorial pieces and on book covers, game boards, and album covers. Deeply rooted in character design, his extremely colorful craziness has its own powerful charm and dynamics. Sami is a recent transplant to Berlin, Germany.

1. **Skinny legged wolves can't jump, 2009**
   Personal
   POSTER • DIGITAL

2. **Skateboarding while drunk, 2009**
   Ruhje Magazine
   EDITORIAL • DIGITAL

3. **Everybody knows that Elvis died of burgers, 2011**
   Personal
   POSTER • DIGITAL

4. **Kai Kai Kitty and the Mysterious Bow Tie, 2010**
   Personal
   POSTER • DIGITAL

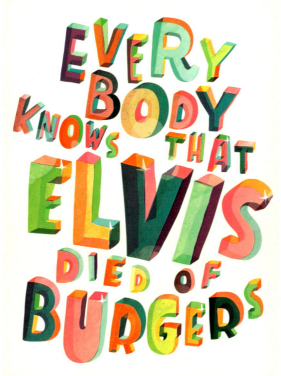

Patrick Hruby

Los Angeles-based illustrator Patrick Hruby grew up in a log cabin within an Idaho forest, and dreamt, as a young boy, of running away to join the circus and becoming a trapeze artist. He grew up to study math and physics before attending the Art Center College of Design, and pursuing a career as an illustrator. His interest in the geometry of nature is central to his work, which uses brilliant colors and crisp shapes. Artists and designers who have influenced him are Charley Harper, Paul Rand, and Mary Blair. His modern aesthetic has won him clients such as the NEW YORK TIMES MAGAZINE, Todd Oldham Studios, AMMO Books, Playboy Jazz Festival, Varsity Pictures, and Brand New School. CMYK MAGAZINE recently named him one of their Top 100 New Creatives.

Scotty Reifsnyder

1. _____ **Heroes of Folk Series**
Personal
LETTERPRESS PRINT

Scotty Reifsnyder pursues projects that utilize his mid-century design and illustration sensibilities. During his time at the award-winning studio Headcase Design, he worked on projects for Eminem, Bravo TV, and the Broadway shows Spring Awakening and Wicked. He has also illustrated for clients such as GQ, TIME MAGAZINE, THE BOSTON GLOBE, THE NEW YORKER, the NEW YORK TIMES, and WIRED. COMMUNICATION ARTS, PRINT MAGAZINE, and AMERICAN ILLUSTRATION have all recognized his work. Most recently, Scotty's HEROES OF FOLK SERIES has been has been selected by the 2011 COMMUNICATION ARTS jury to appear in the ILLUSTRATION ANNUAL 52. In addition to client projects, Reifsnyder teaches illustration and design at the University of Pennsylvania.

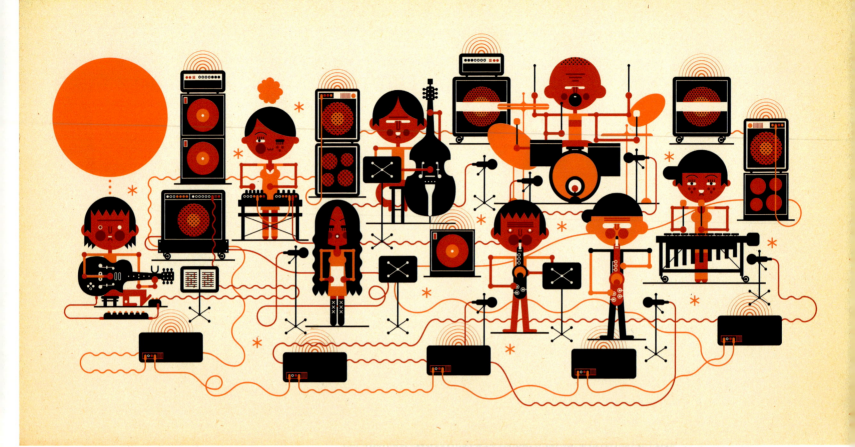

Khuan + Ktron

Khuan+Ktron is a fully equipped graphics studio in Belgium. The studio is dedicated to manufacturing brightly colored printed materials for the arts as well as cultural, educational, and non-profit causes that are in harmony with the rather particular lifestyles of its members, Ningtiendo Sehgah, Steebz a.k.a. ACPL, and Mikail Mitmalka. Their digital illustrations are often highly detailed maps or map-like diagrams of their subjects. Thangka painting, Hieronymus Bosch, anything with Zombies, men in their post-war periods, and the rock-eating madman down the block are just the beginning of a long list of people and things that influence their work.

1. **Onjo - Live at Luchtbal, 2006**
Personal
MURAL DECORATION * DIGITAL
ILLUSTRATOR: NINGTIENDO@KHUAN

2. **Otomotaro 1+2, 2009**
Personal
POSTER * DIGITAL
ILLUSTRATOR: NINGTIENDO@KHUAN

3. **Ski Icons, 2010**
Monocle Magazine
MAGAZINE ICONS * DIGITAL
ILLUSTRATOR: NINGTIENDO@KHUAN

brother · drawing board · amoebae

miso soup · karaoke bar · wanderer

yogi · beefcake · anachronism

gas guzzling coffin · zombie · deadline

OTOMOTARO 2 – TWELVE TERMS FOR FREQUENT USE

boom box · caveman · memory

absolution · wiscac computer · doom

symbiosis · organism · lunch/cannibalism

ecology · vampyr · evolution

OTOMOTARO 1 – TWELVE TERMS FOR FREQUENT USE

MOUNTAIN
RESCUE
HELICOPTER

CARPENTERS

MALL

HOUSE
ALPINE STYLE

RADIO STATION

SKI LIFTS

HOTEL

RADIO MAST

SKIING

RESTAURANT

SNOWBOARDING

BAR

APRES SKI

MOUNTAIN
ANIMALS

MARKET

SOLDIERS
WINTER KIT

Harry Campbell

Before becoming a freelance illustrator for publications such as TIME and the NEW YORK TIMES, Harry Campbell worked for companies such as Nickelodeon and Warner Brothers. The reduced color palette and unique composition of his work is easily recognizable, and has been honored by The Society of Illustrators, COMMUNICATION ARTS, and AMERICAN ILLUSTRATION. He enjoys being outdoors and spending time with his family.

1 _____ **Drop Box, 2011**
MacWorld Magazine
ART DIRECTOR: ROB SCHULTZ
EDITORIAL * DIGITAL

2 _____ **A Plan, 2010**
PlanSponsor Magazine
ART DIRECTOR: SOOJIN BUZELLI
EDITORIAL * DIGITAL

3 _____ **Vending Machine, 2011**
Vend Send Mend
Benefit Exhibition
EXHIBITION PIECE * DIGITAL

4 _____ **Bike Coop, 2010**
Cincinnati Magazine
EDITORIAL * DIGITAL

5 _____ **Chip Tower, 2010**
PC World Magazine
EDITORIAL * DIGITAL

6 _____ **Pegasus Computer, 2010**
University of Miami
EDITORIAL * DIGITAL

7 _____ **Chip, 2010**
IEEE Magazine
EDITORIAL * DIGITAL

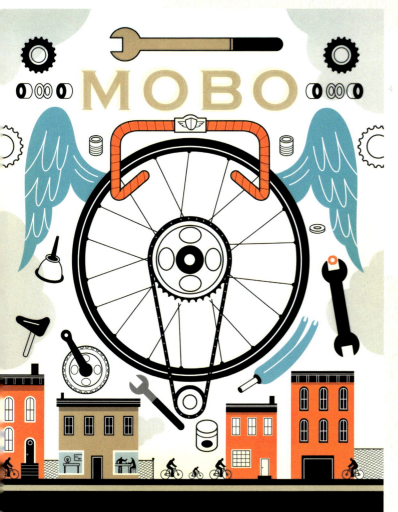

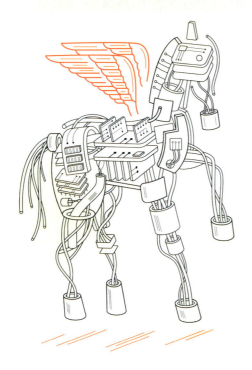

Lotta
Nieminen

Lotta Nieminen is a multidisciplinary designer and illustrator from Helsinki, Finland, now based in New York City. Colorful and rich in textures, her work is always started by hand before being scanned into the computer. She is inspired by a variety of sources including her two cities of New York and Helsinki. Her work has been honored by the Art Directors Club and featured in publications such as the INTERNATIONAL HERALD TRIBUNE MAGAZINE and MONOCLE.

1. **Habitare, 2010**
Habitare
(Finland's biggest annual furniture and design fair)
ADVERTISING * MIXED MEDIA

2. **Children of Alcoholics, 2010**
KODIN KUVALEHTI MAGAZINE, ART DIRECTOR: LEENA PÄLVIÄ
EDITORIAL * MIXED MEDIA

3. **The National, 2010**
The National (band)
ART DIRECTOR: SCOTT DEVENDORF
TOTEBAG * MIXED MEDIA

4. **Helsinki Map, 2010**
Parish Union of Helsinki
ART DIRECTOR: JERE SAULIVAARA
BROCHURE * MIXED MEDIA

5. **Hemispheres, 2010**
United Airlines
ART DIRECTOR: ROB HEWITT
COVER FOR IN-FLIGHT MAGAZINE *
MIXED MEDIA

6. **Global Agenda 2011, 2010**
International
Herald Tribune Magazine
ART DIRECTOR: ERIC JONES
COVER * MIXED MEDIA

GLOBAL AGENDA

NOBROW LTD 62 GREAT EASTERN STREET LONDON EC2A 3QR INFO@NOBROW.NET

Fabrica Grafica

Jan Van Der Veken, a Belgian illustrator, is the force behind the design studio Fabrica Grafica. His style, a derivative of the Atomic style—a 1980s interpretation of Ligne claire—can be seen on book covers and posters, and in a variety of newspapers and magazines, including THE NEW YORKER.

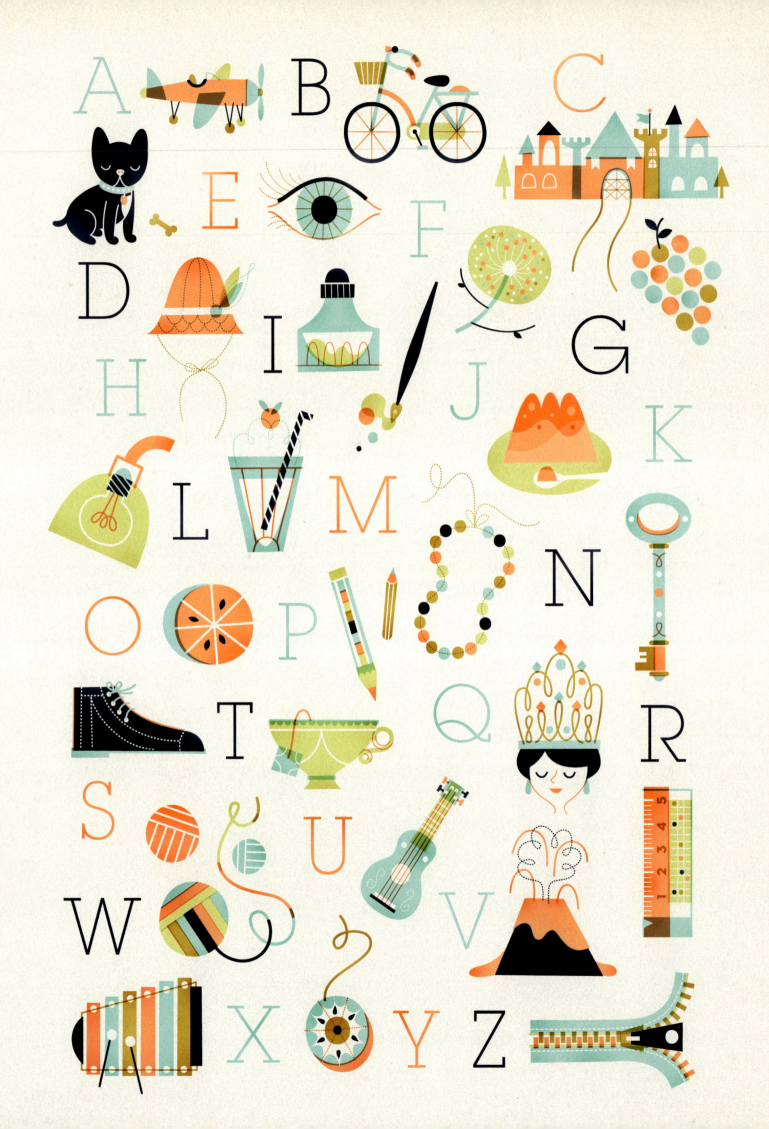

Sol Linero

Sol Linero was born in San Miguel del Monte, Argentina. She later moved to Buenos Aires to study graphic design, a career that would lead her to the world of motion graphics and later to illustration. It was when Sol moved the United States to work for MTV Latin America that she discovered her fascination for vintage illustration.
After returning to Buenos Aires, she founded her own design studio and now counts Nickelodeon, the Discovery Channel, VH1, and Unicef amongst her clients.
Her favorite sources of inspiration include the work of Charley Harper, Marc Boutavant, Juliana Pedemonte, and Jesse Lefkowitz.

Blanca Gómez

Blanca Gómez lives and works in her hometown of Madrid, Spain, producing work that has been featured in numerous magazines, advertising campaigns, and exhibitions. During her studies, she explored photography and film before discovering graphic design in Milan at an exhibition of the work of Milton Glaser. Her work as an illustrator has been influenced by the French illustrator Sempé as well as the comics illustrators Dupuy and Barberian, and the Japanese illustrator Tatsuro Kiuchi. Mid-century designers, such as Alexander Girad, Olle Eksell, and Bruno Munari, have also played a large part in the development of her style. The printing techniques of Catalonian studio Vostok are a current inspiration, as is the work of illustrator and designer Cristobal Schmal.

Zara Picken

Zara Picken is a Bristol-based Illustrator who creates digital illustrations for editorial, advertising, and publishing. She finds inspiration in vast collections, large cities, literature, and obscure music and is influenced by mid-century modern design and paper-based ephemera. Her work, which is retro-tinted with textured blocks of color, combines digital and handmade elements, and begins with pencil drawings that are completed using Digital. Her clients include THE GUARDIAN, The National Trust, Macmillan Publishing, WIRED, and LONELY PLANET MAGAZINE.

1. **Starman, 2010**
   Personal
   DIGITAL

2. **The Queen's Birthday, 2010**
   Personal
   DIGITAL

3. **Photographic Memory, 2010**
   Personal
   POSTCARD * DIGITAL

4. **Tiramisu, 2011**
   Personal
   POSTER * DIGITAL

5. **Hair Loss, 2011**
   St. Louis Magazine
   ART DIRECTOR: DANNY ELCHERT
   EDITORIAL * DIGITAL

Jesse LeDoux

1. _____ **Summer, 2010**
Personal
INK | GOUACHE

2. | 3. _____ **Perfect**
Forecast 3 & 5, 2010
Schmancy Gallery
INK | GOUACHE

Born in Portland, Oregon, Jesse LeDoux worked for many years as an art director for Seattle-based Sub Pop Records, where he created the Grammy-nominated album packaging for The Shins's album CHUTES TOO NARROW. Since 2004, he has pursued commercial and personal work at his studio, LeDouxville, and will be opening a pop-up gallery and retail space later this year. Some influences on his work include old cartoons, Ben Shahn, Miroslav Sasek, Tim Biskup, Paul Rand, Alex Steinweiss, Walker Evans, and Henri Cartier-Bresson. He currently lives and works in Seattle.

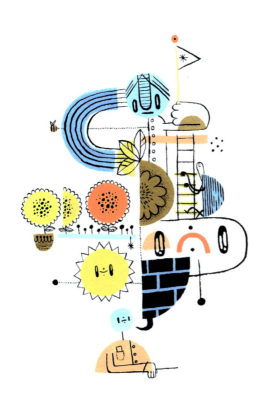

WHAT WAS IT ABOUT GROWING UP AROUND PORTLAND THAT INFLUENCED YOUR STYLE OR CONTENT? I think most kids grow up drawing. For some, their interests shift toward other things—sports, video games, fire—as they get older, while others never lose that desire to create. I fall into the latter category. I grew up on several acres 30 minutes outside of Portland so my childhood was largely spent either outside exploring the woods behind the house, or inside with a pile of crayons, markers, and paper. Both exploration and the desire to create are two things I've never been able to shake.

DO YOU REMEMBER—OR CAN YOU DESCRIBE—WHO YOUR EARLY INSPIRATIONS AND INFLUENCES WERE? I was raised on a steady diet of Disney. We took family vacations to Disneyland every couple of years, which had a significant impact on me. As I got older, I discovered MAD, the suspiciously similar CRACKED, and CARTOONS magazines, where I discovered folks like Mort Drucker, Dan Clowes, and Shawn Kerri. That should have lead me to underground comics like Clowes's EIGHTBALL and all the great stuff Fantagraphics was publishing, but living in the boonies in the late 1980s and early 1990s with parents who had no interest in driving me to Portland eliminated that chance. Instead, I was at the mercy of whatever the magazine rack at the grocery store had in stock. This led me to the skateboard magazine THRASHER, which was a pivotal discovery for me. Although it was a skateboarding magazine, they featured so much more than skateboarding—music, art, films… culture! Granted, it wasn't "culture" in the traditional sense, but it was a lot more than I was able to access otherwise. From the pages of THRASHER, I was able to make lists of bands or books to check out the next time I made it to Portland.

WHILE WE'RE ON THE SUBJECT OF INFLUENCE, HOW DID YOUR MOVE TO TOKYO CHANGE OR EVOLVE YOUR PROCESS? Living in Tokyo affected me far deeper than I'd ever imagined. I don't know if it changed how I create my work, as much as the reasons why I create. Prior to Japan, I was interested in ideas of escapism and creating imaginary creatures, and an alternate universe I could lose myself in. However, Japan quickly deflated those aspirations by showing me that the utopian landscape I had been working so hard to create already exists—and it's only an ocean away! (Even Tokyo's police department has a whimsical, sprite-like mascot, Pipo-kun, keeping the residents of Tokyo safe.) Then, I began to notice the subtle balance within Japanese culture: centuries-old temples right next to high-tech skyscrapers; vending machines selling coffee, ice cream, even clothing while just a couple doors down, a man hand-makes soba noodles in the window of his restaurant. The contrasts couldn't be more different, yet they worked together seamlessly. I began to think about balance in a larger scale and how the desire to achieve equilibrium is fundamental to humans—hot versus cold, work versus play, quadruple-bacon cheeseburger versus healthy salad. Since my time in Japan, my work has explored the various facets of balance, both aesthetically and conceptually.

CAN YOU DESCRIBE THE STEPS YOU TAKE TO CREATE AN IMAGE? If the image I'm creating is for commercial purposes, I'll typically spend several days thinking about the client's needs and desires before touching pencil to paper. Most often, I'll build the image in my head; mentally trying various possibilities until I have something I think will work well for their needs. From there, my goal is to try my best to recreate the image I see in my head. Because the tactile aesthetic is important to me, I draw the elements of the image out separately and use the computer to build my images. Working digitally in this way makes it far easier if the client requests any changes while also retaining a hand-done look. For personal work, as in the case of a gallery show, I will think of both an overarching theme to the body of work, and an overview of how the gallery installation will look. Once I have a solid direction for the body of work, I set goals for the number of pieces and get to work. For the majority of my gallery work, I've been using ink and gouache on thick Arches cold press watercolor paper. I do the gouache shapes first, without much pre-planning other than having the predominant theme at the forethought of my mind. Once the shapes and colors have the proper rhythm and balance, I draw the ink line work on top. It all comes together rather instinctively—in a way, it draws itself. I don't use the computer for any of my gallery work. That's cheating.

WHAT'S THE RELATIONSHIP BETWEEN THE HAND-DRAWN AND DIGITAL ELEMENTS OF YOUR IMAGES? Unless I want a very clean, perfect shape (which is rare), I'll hand-draw my elements. The majority of most digitally generated images lacks a soul and generally feel a bit cold and empty. However, the computer is an essential tool in contemporary illustration. I use it primarily in coloring the image, since that's usually the final stage in the design process, and the part that requires the most tweaking to satisfy the client.

THERE SEEMS TO BE SOME NEW FORMAL CHARACTERISTICS IN THE NEWER PERSONAL WORK. IS IT DIFFERENT PRIMARILY BECAUSE IT'S PERSONAL WORK OR DO YOU PLAN TO INCORPORATE IT INTO YOUR COMMERCIAL WORK AS WELL? This work, with formal geometric shapes and overlaid organic line work, first started out as personal work only. I've since had a few clients request this style. Because my approach toward client and personal work are quite different, it's honestly been a bit tricky to achieve a similar result. The latest instance of a client wanting this style was for the 2011 Bumbershoot festival graphics. I had to dissect my approach and reverse-engineer it so I would be able to build it digitally to allow for client modifications.

SO WHAT'S YOUR ALL-TIME FAVORITE THING TO DRAW? Clouds have been my longtime muse. They're always different, their meaning can be interpreted as both good and bad, and are hard to draw wrong.

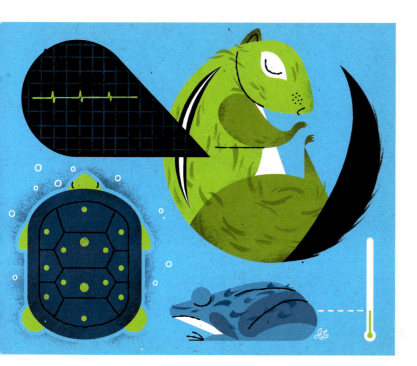

Jesse Lefkowitz

1. **Making Money in 2011, 2010**
   Money Magazine
   ART DIRECTION: TOM O'QUINN
   EDITORIAL * DIGITAL

2. **Hibernation, 2011**
   The Washington Post
   ART DIRECTION: ALLISON GHAMAN
   EDITORIAL * DIGITAL

3. **Cuban Jazz, 2011**
   The Village Voice
   ART DIRECTION: JOHN DIXON
   COVER * DIGITAL

4. **Lion, 2010**
   Personal
   POSTER * DIGITAL

5. **Bull, 2010**
   Personal
   POSTER * DIGITAL

California-based artist Jesse Lefkowitz creates illustrations for a wide range of magazines, newspapers, and other media. He works from his home studio in Berkeley using pencils, gouache, and Photoshop to make work with a vintage feel, and reduced color palette for publications such as ROLLING STONE, THE NEW YORKER, and the TIMES.

Øivind Hovland

Øivind Hovland, the author of two illustrated books published by Tabella, has been short-listed for IMAGES 31 and the Nationwide Mercury Prize Art Exhibition. Screen printing has long been his medium of choice and its aesthetic can been seen in all of his work, whether it be digital or handmade, which he creates for advertising, editorial, and publishing projects.

His clients include THE INDEPENDENT, SUNDAY TELEGRAPH, TIME OUT MAGAZINE, Random House, RADIO TIMES, HMRC, and ESQUIRE. He lives and works in Bristol, U.K.

Till Hafenbrak

German illustrator Till Hafenbrak uses a limited color palette to create detailed images from blocks of solid colors. His work has been featured in magazines and albums.

Alexis Rom ::: Atelier Vostok

1–5 **Un Sedicesimo 19b, 2010**
Corraini
BOOK * SCREENPRINT

Alexis Rom studied graphic design in Barcelona and New York City. Together with Claude Marzotto, he runs Alexis Rom Estudio ::: Atelier Vostok, a workshop for ideas, graphics, and illustration based in Barcelona, Spain, and Milan, Italy. They work in different fields of visual communication in the spirit of a creative studio, mixing graphic languages, techniques, and methods for advertising, editorial, apparel, and branding.

Blexbolex

Known for his willingness to experiment with illustration and printing techniques, book illustrator and cartoonist Blexbolex has made a name for himself with his children's books and graphic novels for Thierry Magnier, Cornélius, and Pipifax, among others. Born Bernard Granger in Douai, France, in 1966, he moved to Aurillac before attending school in Angoulême. He eventually moved to Berlin, Germany, where he worked at the Kunsthochschule Berlin-Weissensee. During the 2009 Leipzig Book Fair, he was honored with the award for the best book design in the world for his work on L'Imagier Des Gens (2008). He lives, works, and teaches in Leipzig.

UN **É T É**

HOW DID YOU FIRST GET INTERESTED IN DRAWING AND ILLUSTRATION? My father was interested in art, drawing, cartoons, and comics. He would buy us kids comics besides the regular children's books, read them for us, and he sometimes did drawings inspired by Tintin, Mickey Mouse, or others. It was a lot of fun for him, and it made us happy as children. I tried to draw as soon as I was able. Then in the late 1970s I met a friend who was producing his own comics, and we did a few together. It was a time for fanzines, so it was rather easy to borrow the Xerox machine at school and publish them. One day, my friend's older brother secretly brought an issue of MÉTAL HURLANT (Heavy Metal) to school. It was a shock and a revelation at the same time, like being transported to modernity in a moment.

WHAT WAS IT THAT CAUSED SUCH A REVELATION? It was intelligent comics for adults. My friend and I were looking to do science-fiction comics. And in this magazine were among the best comics artists of the time, and Moebius was the best of them. But there was also Nicollet, Druillet, Kelek, Tardi, and later Corben and many others, who were producing something absolutely new, very far from our country-boy lives. It was the mix of exotic, violence, and sexuality, of course, that attracted us, but the aesthetics were really impressive too. I remember a special issue about Ridley Scott's film ALIEN —science fiction had never looked so realistic. It's hard to translate how I felt at that moment, but it was like a signal: the future was here, and happening now.

DID YOU FIRST START SCREENPRINTING WHILE YOU WERE IN SCHOOL? My first print was an etching. I was enthusiastic about it, but the use of color, and the slowness of the process, was a real problem. I wanted to try a lot of things, but the place was filled with older students who were preparing work for their diploma, and you could sometimes wait weeks for a printing machine. I didn't like the silkscreen printing technique at first. I found it complicated, noisy, and stinky, and the screens are expensive and fragile. And then the cleaning, with special glasses, gas mask and protective equipment for your ears, made me nervous. I finally printed maybe two posters but finally abandoned it, and worked on something else.

I GOT A MEMO TWO DAYS AGO VIA SPYPHONE, NON-SCHEDULED ABDUCTION OF DOGFRIEND. SYMBIOTIC PERSONNEL DISINCLINED TO DISCLOSE NON-ANONYMITY. I CAN'T REMEMBER THE LAST TIME I GOT A TELEBRIEF BY SPYPHONE, THE WHOLE SET-UP JUST REEKS OF BIG MONEY!

THE DIRECTOR OF THE DOGS' HOME CONFIRMS THAT, LAURA, A BITCHFRIEND OF UNCERTAIN PEDIGREE, HAS GONE MISSING. HASN'T SHOWN UP ALL WEEK AND DIDN'T TAKE PART IN THE TAIL REFLEXOLOGY SESSION THAT THE CANINE UNION HAD SIGNED HER UP FOR (APPARENTLY IT'S NOT EASY TO GET A PLACE).

EINE GROSSE FABRIK AM SAUM DES DSCHUNGELS IST ALLES, WAS ZU SEHEN IST. DIE STRASSE FÜHRT NICHT WEITER – WIE UNHEIMLICH. –„ICH FRAGE MICH, WAS DA DRIN IST, SOLLEN WIR MAL REINGEHEN?" ANDERERSEITS HABE ICH KEINE LUST DARAUF. ICH WILL NUR SO SCHNELL WIE MÖGLICH UNSEREN KANINCHENSTALL FINDEN UND MICH LANG MACHEN. ICH BIN WIE ERSCHLAGEN. DIE LUFT IST PRAKTISCH NICHT MEHR ZU ATMEN. –. VIELLEICHT MORGEN … UND DANN HAUEN WIR HIER SO SCHNELL WIE MÖGLICH WIEDER AB."

DIE TÜR DES BUNGALOWS SCHLIESST SICH AUTOMATISCH HINTER UNS, DAS LICHT SCHALTET UM 22 UHR 15 AUF NACHTLICHT UND DIE VIDEOKAMERAS IN DEN INFRAROT-MODUS. UM 22 UHR 30 ZIEHEN WIR UNSERE MASKEN ÜBER, UM DEN GERUCH ZU VERGESSEN. UM 23 UHR ERKLÄRT UNS EINE STIMME MIT SELTSAMEM AKZENT DIE RECHTE UND PFLICHTEN EINES NEUEN BÜRGERS. DAS IST DIE VON UNSEREM GUTEN MEISTER, DEM DOKTOR PRAXIS. UM MITTERNACHT SCHWEIGT DIE STIMME ENDLICH. ICH DENKE, DIE NACHT WIRD KURZ.

WHEN DID YOU PICK IT BACK UP? After school, I went to Paris, living with friends or relatives, with no place to work. I had to abandon all my pretentions in art or else. That's how I started to draw, because it doesn't need so much space. You can draw anywhere, in the subway, during lunchtime, and that's what I did, to breathe, to have my own room, exactly like when I was a child.

A friend of mine was working in a print shop, and they needed help for some extra work, so I started and stayed there almost two years. This friend had seen my drawings and suggested to do a book with them—it was my very first one, and while doing it, I learned almost everything I know about how to do a book. The book sold well, and so I thought, okay, if they want this, I'll keep doing it.

WAS THIS WHEN YOU DEVELOPED YOUR OWN VERSION OF THE LIGNE CLAIRE STYLE? I did a lot of silkscreen-printed self-publications and the technique itself forced me to simplify my forms and use better masses of colors instead of fine lines, because I was never sure about the machine or the screens I was going to use. They could be really bad sometimes. I did my first illustrated children's book in 2000. It was painful. I created the illustrations for the whole book five or six times over and over again. I was never satisfied, and I came to the conclusion that the main problem was the kind of thick brush outlines I was using.

WERE YOU INFLUENCED AT ALL BY TINTIN AND SERGE CLERC? Yes of course, I liked the drawings of Serge Clerc during the 1980s, which was done in this style, but I liked them for other reasons—because it was like rock'n' roll translated into comics, something rather exciting at the time. But Charles Burns and Gary Panter were and still are a more important influence for me and my drawings. And I really went to this style when I discovered, first, the books of Richard McGuire, and then met the artist himself. It left me with an impression of simplicity and complexity at the same time, control and freedom, with strong artistic references and a wild, or at least unexpected, inspiration. All in all, a paradox.

WHEN DID YOU DISCOVER BURNS AND PANTER? I discovered them during the beginning of the 1990s. I bought JIMBO, ADVENTURES IN PARADISE in New York without even really looking at it. I just wanted to bring back home something from NYC. And then I forgot about it until I really read it a few months later and it was a total shock. I couldn't believe it existed. I borrowed Charles Burns's EL BORBAH from the public library and was captivated because it's so cold, nasty, and funny. My admiration for Charles's work grew more slowly, but constantly and continuously until today.

LE FOUTU RAFIOT N'EST QU'UNE COQUE AUTISTE. TOUT CE QUI AURAIT PU SERVIR À LA NAVIGATION EST DÉTRUIT, CE QUI EN SOI NE ME FAIT NI CHAUD NI FROID, VU QUE JE NE SAIS PAS ME SERVIR DE CES TRUCS-LÀ. C'EST BIEN PARTI POUR LA LONGUE DÉRIVE, ALORS JE M'INSTALLE DANS MES NOUVEAUX QUARTIERS. JE N'AI AUCUN PLAN. DEPUIS QUAND BRÈVE BASCULE DANS MON PETIT GOUFFRE PERSONNEL.

LA LECTURE DU LIVRE DE BORD M'APPREND PAS GRAND-CHOSE. DES RAPPORTS MÉTÉO, L'ÉTAT DE LA MER ET LES MENUS INCIDENTS DU QUOTIDIEN DE L'ÉQUIPAGE, DES DATES D'ESCALES, DES LISTES DE LIVRAISONS À N'EN PLUS FINIR ET LE TEMPS QUI REFUSE DE PASSER. QUEL TEMPS?

- 5 -
FISH

AND WAS THAT ABOUT THE SAME TIME WHEN YOU CAME ACROSS THE WORK OF RICHARD MCGUIRE? No. I saw Richard's books later, in 1998 maybe, when I was working for Cornélius. The Orange Book and What's Wrong With This Book? and Night Becomes Day. And found the same feeling again, modernity, something eye-catching with a meaning. But also something very different, a lack of any aggression, something kind, friendly, and touching, something done for children, but with an adult's point of view, poetic but never condescending or pretentious. Richard's drawings are in fact as radical as the ones by Gary Panter, but in a very different tradition, more European, maybe. My own feeling is that time plays a big role in Richard's works—they've always got perfect timing.

WHAT IS YOUR PROCESS LIKE WHEN STARTING A BOOK? Starting a book means that I will sit for hours, days, weeks, or months (and sometimes years!) in front of my computer. The first thing I need is an idea that makes me enthusiastic enough. Inspiration comes from everywhere, the street, what I see from my window or while I'm sitting in a café, things I'm reading in books, newspapers or the internet, music, films. It must reach a sort of critical mass, and sometimes it comes without even looking for it. Sometimes it needs a lot of time and work. When I did my first silkscreen-printed books, I wanted them to be colorful. I came to a kind of basic four-color process, printing the fewest colors to obtain the maximal effect in combining them, using just the transparency of the ink. With only three flat-printed colors, you've actually got eight or nine if you consider the paper as a ground-color. You can express a lot of things in nine colors, and you can create a lot of different atmospheres. In fact, it's almost all I need. Then, you can refine it, using rasters that create halftones on each color, and a graphic effect as well. It's nothing new, as you can see, but it is still fascinating to me. This search for the maximal effect with minimal means is a good exercise for the mind, satisfying and playful at the same time.

WOULD YOU SAY THIS SEARCH FOR "MAXIMAL EFFECT WITH MINIMAL MEANS" IS AN OVERARCHING PHILOSOPHY OF YOUR WORK? OR IS IT MAINLY A FINANCIAL CONSIDERATION? This is difficult to answer. Money doesn't play such a big role in the artistic direction. You clearly need money to work in good conditions, and with more money, you can maybe have the best material you need and maybe the best people, but what else? If there are too many things to manage at the same time, I feel a little lost. The game seems more interesting when you've got limitations. I like the feeling of discovering other possibilities with the same simple, basic things and push them as far as I can. And though economy is interesting in an artistic point of view, but I wouldn't make it an ideology. I try to do simple things, to make them as well as I can, and that is difficult enough.

Iv Orlov

Iv Orlov is
an illustrator
based in Murmansk, Russia.

1. **Biotechnologies, 2008**
   Facecontrol (Russia),
   POSTER * DIGITAL

2. **Piano, 2008**
   Men's Health magazine
   (RUSSIA)
   PHOTO EDITOR: ROMAN VOROPAEV
   EDITORIAL * DIGITAL

3. **Robot, 2010**
   CEO magazine (RUSSIA)
   ART DIRECTOR: ROMAN MANICHIN
   EDITORIAL * DIGITAL

4. **Missoni, 2009**
   Personal
   INTERIOR POSTER * DIGITAL

5. **Alzheimer, 2008**
Men's Health magazine
(RUSSIA)
PHOTO EDITOR: ROMAN VOROPAEV
MAGAZINE ILLUSTRATION * DIGITAL

6. **Ritmolider, 2008**
Mellophonia Records
ALBUM COVER * DIGITAL

7. **Animal-robots, 2009**
HalfBag (RUSSIA)
BAG * DIGITAL

Roman Klonek

Roman Klonek was born in Kattowitz, Poland. He came to Düsseldorf, Germany to study and there discovered a passion for woodcut printing. He has a soft spot for old-fashioned East European cartoons and creates posters whose whimsical animal/half human creatures in awkward situations strike a balance between propaganda, folklore, and pop.
He works together with friends in a studio in Düsseldorf, Germany.

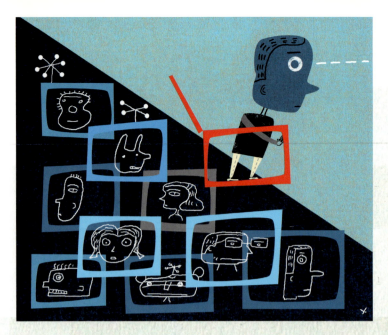

James Yang

James Yang was born and raised in Oklahoma, but now calls New York City home. The early influences on his work were Saul Steinberg, Ralph Steadman, and Joan Miró.

Since he began his career in 1983, Yang's work has changed over the years, though it is possible to see a thread; he currently enjoys the work of Tim Biskup as well as retro images from the 1950s and early 1960s. His illustration and design work has been featured in numerous design annuals, and won countless awards. Top publishers and clients using his work including Atheneum Books / Simon & Schuster, FORBES, Herman Miller, the NEW YORK TIMES, and the Smithsonian Institution. Yang has taught and lectured at colleges and universities around the world.

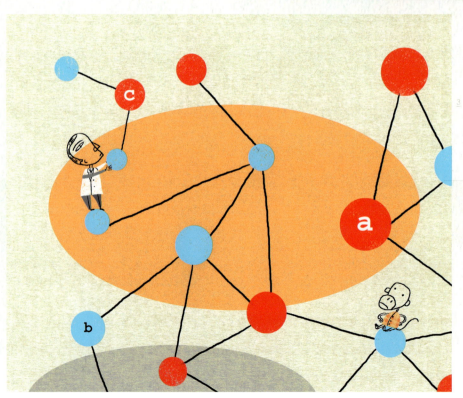

Ben Newman

A Bristol-based illustrator who has exhibited his work internationally, Ben Newman is known for his contemporary fusion of bold shapes, bright colors, and playful characters. He has produced work for clients including the Tate, Fantagraphics, Selfridges London, and Magma Books. Ben has worked with Nobrow on various projects, including his own comic book OUROBOROS.

His work has been described as "fuzzy-felt Bauhaus folk illustration."

1. **Art Attack!, 2009**
Tate Modern,
POSTER * HAND DRAWN | DIGITAL

2. **Bishop's O'O', 2011**
Ghost Of Gone Birds,
EXHIBTION PRINT *
HAND DRAWN | DIGITAL

3. **The Digital Divide, 2010**
Teaching Tolerance
EDITORIAL * HAND DRAWN | DIGITAL

4.|5.|6. **Mask:
Two, Four, Six, 2011**
Personal
PRINT SERIES * HAND DRAWN | DIGITAL

7. **A Few of My
Favourite Things, 2011**
Nobrow Press
WRAPPING PAPER * HAND DRAWN |
DIGITAL

Alberto Cerriteño

Alberto Cerriteño is a Mexican illustrator and designer who lives in Portland, USA. Strongly inspired by urban vinyl toys, alternative cartoons, and the pop surrealism movement, Alberto Cerriteño has developed his own technique and style; he combines delicate hints of traditional Mexican artistic influences with his own rich textures and decorative patterns. These contrast strikingly with a blend of desaturated colors and ink. Cerriteño's illustrations have been recognized by progressive art institutions such as Juxtapoz, Create, Drawn!, Computer Arts, and Communication Arts among others. He has also been invited to participate in collaborative art projects all around the world as well as solo, and group shows.

Michael Mullan

A native of Chicago, Michael Mullan is now based out of rural Vermont, where he roams the rolling hills to pull inspiration from nature, memories of his suburban upbringing, and 1950s and 1960s pop culture. Artists Andy Warhol and Jean Dubuffet, as well as the traditions of folk, outsider, and children's art can also be seen as inspirations to his work. He uses digital and traditional techniques blended with simple shapes and colors to create a graphic, handmade style that captures a quality of childlike simplicity and imperfection. His work has been used for magazine editorials, advertising, package design, and featured in AMERICAN ILLUSTRATION 28. When not at work, Mullan can be found running through the back woods, sitting by a hot grill, sipping on a tasty home brew, and listening to The Beatles.

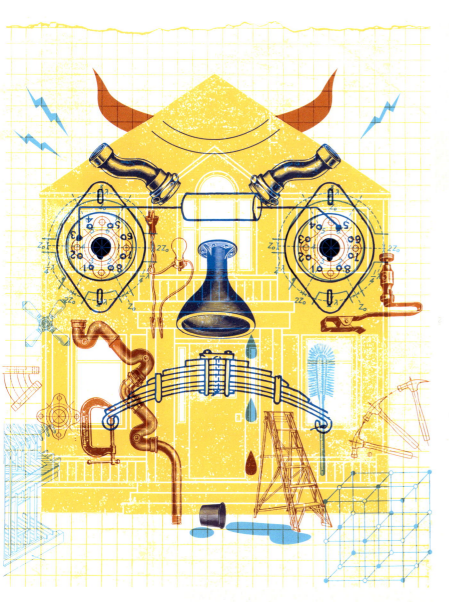

Carl Wiens

The projects taken on by Carl Wiens in his studio practice have included magazines, books, character development for animation, and labels for wine and beer makers. His work, which is largely digitally produced, centers around themes of machinery and nature, and has been used by the New York Times, Esquire, the Wall Street Journal, and Time. He lives and works in Prince Edward County, Ontario, in a small barn that houses a fleet of bicycles on the first floor, and a big bright studio on the second floor.

Jeff Kulak

Pencil, ink, and vectors are the tools of choice for Canadian illustrator Jeff Kulak, who makes his home in Montreal. Inspiration for his work comes by way of drawing with children, watching a beautifully shot film, mountains, music, coffee, bikes, books, and making screen prints. His work has appeared in print many times, most notably in books such as ALPHABET BOYS, and the recently released LEARN TO SPEAK MUSIC.

1._____ **Tiger Library, 2011**
The National Post
COVER * INK, GRAPHITE, DIGITAL

2._____ **Ted Leo &**
the Brutalist Bricks, 2010
Beatroute Magazine
EDITORIAL * SPRAYPAINT, DIGITAL

5

6

Riccardo Guasco

Illustrator and art director Riccardo Guasco was born in Piedmont, Italy. He now works from Casale Monferrato, where he paints what surrounds him including tall houses, bicycles, large whales, migratory birds, boats, and clouds. His work, which uses a combination of materials and tools such as watercolor, acrylic paint, and the computer, has a cubist feel to it. He counts his influences as Picasso, Munari, Rodari, Malevich, and Basquiat.

1._____ **Corvo colto, 2010**
Personal
POSTER * DIGITAL

2._____ **Fatal Dribbling, 2011**
Personal
POSTER * DIGITAL

3._____ **La morte,**
la maschera e il corvo,
2011
www.nurant.it
POSTER * DIGITAL

4._____ **Balenare, 2010**
Personal
POSTER * DIGITAL

5.___ **La balena e il pino, 2010**
Personal
POSTER * DIGITAL

6._____ **Pensieri al guinzaglio,**
2010
Personal
POSTER * DIGITAL

7.___ **Per un soffio le farfalle,**
2010
Personal
POSTER * DIGITAL

Laszlito Kovac

Laszlito Kovac lives and works 1699 km from his home in Amsterdam, Netherlands. He crafts colorful and optimistic illustrations, and animations that have been published in international newspapers and magazines such as EL PAÍS, EL MUNDO, BRIGHT MAGAZINE, WWF PANDA MAGAZINE, ADOBE CS5 MAGAZIN, and DE VOLKSKRANT. In addition to being an artist, Kovac is a curator at Poolga.com and the chief editor at Endtopic.com. He finds his inspiration in the work of animator and illustrator Chuck Jones, movies, music, pigs, deer, whales, penguins, and all things that make this world sweet, and better.

1.   **Poolga Wallpapers, 2010/2011**
Poolga.com
WALLPAPER * DIGITAL

2.   **2046 Alternative Cover, 2010**
Henry Pierrot
EXPOSED BOOK COVER * DIGITAL

3.   **Space Drift, 2010**
Personal
IPAD COVER * DIGITAL

4.   **The Teleportation Paradox, 2010**
Personal
POSTER, IPAD COVER * DIGITAL

5.   **2046 , 2010**
Henry Pierrot
BOOK COVER * DIGITAL

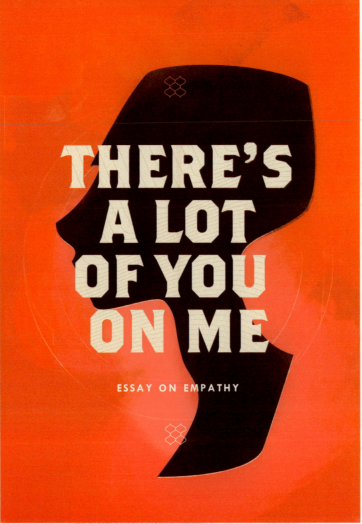

THERE'S A LOT OF YOU ON ME

ESSAY ON EMPATHY

LOVE
INSPIRES

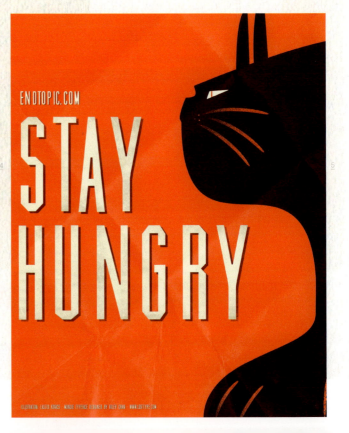

SÓLO RESTABA SUMERGIRSE
EN AQUEL MAR QUE AMENAZABA
CON ANIQUILARME

NI RASTRO ALGUNO
DEL ROSTRO AMADO

CERRADA YA LA NOCHE CON CANDADO
SIN SILENCIOSAS ESTELAS DE AEROPLANOS
QUE PUDIERAN DELATAR MIS ESTÚPIDOS ACTOS

TODO DEBERÁ SUCEDER ASÍ...
LA MÍNIMA RÁFAGA DE LUZ
LES SERÁ SUFICIENTE

PERO AHORA ACÉRCAME TU
CARA, COLÓCALA SOBRE LA MÍA

CORRÍA EL AÑO 2046 CUANDO
VOLVIERON A DESPERTARME

CUANDO DESPERTÉ
NADA QUEDABA YA DEL SER HUMANO

TODAS ESAS LUCES DE NEÓN (JAPONÉS)
PROYECTANDO FUNESTAS SOMBRAS (CHINAS)

Eoin Ryan

Eoin Ryan is an Irish illustrator and animator based in London, U.K. His work, once described by Nick Talbot from the band Gravenhurst as "pastoral Soviet Block," has a wide variety of influences: Japanese woodblock art by Hokusai and Kuniyoshi, old Chinese maps and acupuncture diagrams, Haida Indian art, M.C. Escher, architectural drawings, information graphics, Isotype, and propaganda art. Although his final work is always digital, his process begins with pencil, ink, and textures from old paper in an attempt to ingrain a handmade quality into the final piece. His recent clients include WALLPAPER*, GQ, NEW SCIENTIST, and WIRED MAGAZINE.

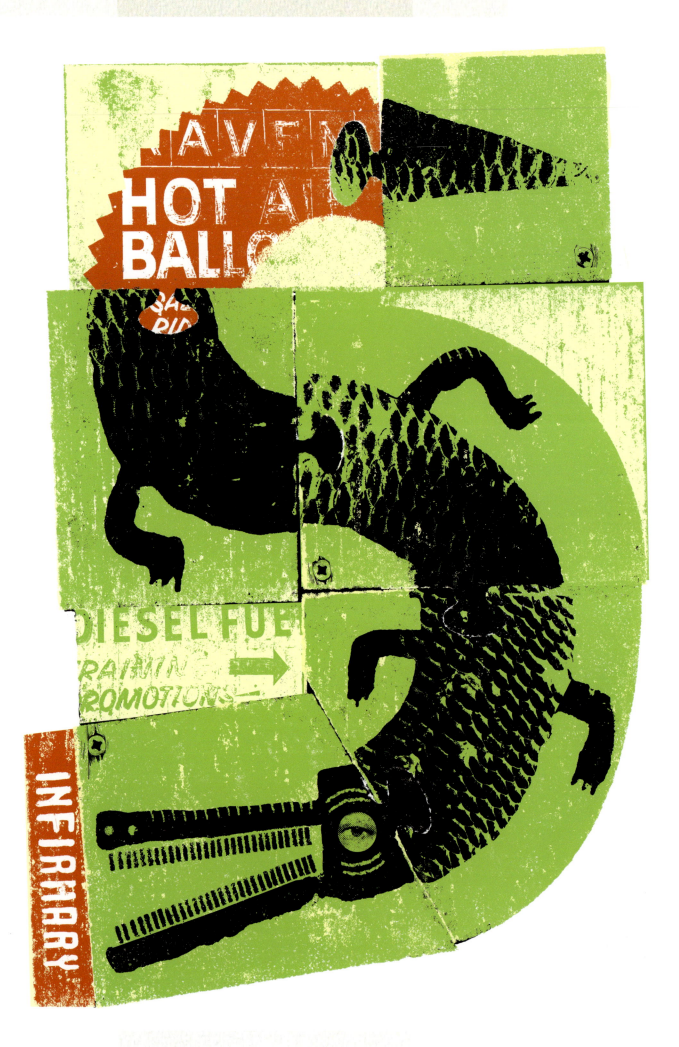

Curt Merlo

Affinities with pop art, comic books, retro commercialism, and anything mid-century modern, or minimalist are evident in Curt Merlo's work. He began his career as an art student, then moved into graphic design, and finally into illustration. His clients include SCIENTIFIC AMERICAN, LA WEEKLY, OC WEEKLY, DALLAS OBSERVER, and the VILLAGE VOICE. Illustrators such as Lotta Nimenen, Raymond Beisinger, and Charlie Harper have provided inspiration for his work as well as ads, posters, and toys from twentieth century America. He lives and works in Costa Mesa, California.

David Plunkert

Dave Plunkert's illustrations have appeared in advertising campaigns for Fortune 500 companies as well as major newspapers, magazines, and recording labels. He uses two styles, collage and a blocky technique, to create work that has been recognized by American Illustration, the Society of Illustrators, and The New York Art Director's Club. He has been featured in numerous books and taught and lectured at various institutions in the United States. His work has been collected by museums and private collectors, and exhibited internationally. He lives and works in Baltimore, USA.

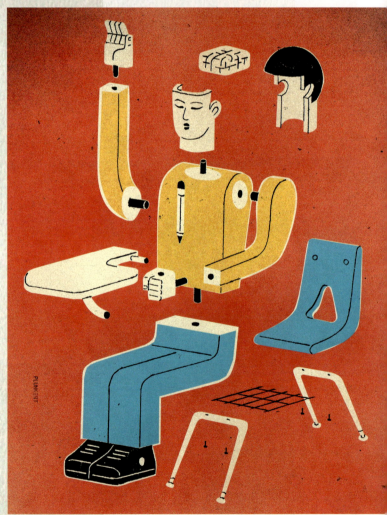

1._____**The White Anxiety Crisis, 2010**
Time Magazine
ART DIRECTOR: TOM MILLER
EDITORIAL * MIXED MEDIA | DIGITAL

2._____**The 5 Biggest Health Risks for Men: Bad Habits, 2011**
5280 Magazine
ART DIRECTOR: DAVE MCKENNA
EDITORIAL * MIXED MEDIA | DIGITAL

3._____**A Snapshot of Human Mating Habits in the Digital Age, 2011**
Playboy
ART DIRECTOR: CODY TILSON
EDITORIAL * MIXED MEDIA | DIGITAL

4.__**The Model Student, 2010**
Educause
ART DIRECTOR: JEFF KIBLER
EDITORIAL * MIXED MEDIA | DIGITAL

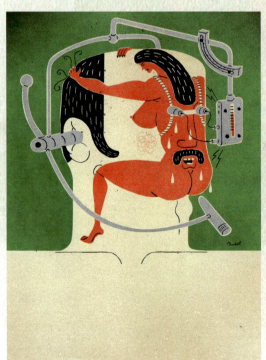

5 _____ **Belt Tightening in the
New Economy, 2008**
Inc. Magazine
ART DIRECTOR: SARAH GARCEA
EDITORIAL * MIXED MEDIA | DIGITAL

6 _____ **The 5 Biggest Health
Risks for Men:
Prostate Cancer, 2011**
5280 Magazine
ART DIRECTOR: DAVE MCKENNA
EDITORIAL * MIXED MEDIA | DIGITAL

7 _____ **The Overweight
Stigma, 2006**
Dallas Morning News
ART DIRECTOR: MICHAEL HOGUE
EDITORIAL * MIXED MEDIA | DIGITAL

8 _____ **The 5 Biggest Health
Risks for Men:
Heart Attack, 2011**
5280 Magazine
ART DIRECTOR: DAVE MCKENNA
EDITORIAL * MIXED MEDIA | DIGITAL

Adam Hancher

The moody, vintage atmosphere of Adam Hancher's illustrations finds its inspiration in the limited-color palettes of 1920s and 1930s graphic design, the minute details of engravers such as Thomas Bewick, and folk tales and stories of eras gone by—firefighters stationed in the American wilderness in the early 1900s, Native American and pioneer legends and Icelandic mythology. Utagawa Hiroshige, Hieronymous Bosch, and Diego Rivera are several artists who he counts as influences, and he has recently taken an interest in Snorri Sturluson's classic Norse text THE PROSE EDDA. His work has been used in editorial illustrations for WIRED and GQ MAGAZINES, YCN, animated videos, and posters. He lives and works in Bristol, England.

WHERE DID YOU GROW UP? I grew up in a town called Sedgley, which is in the West Midlands, near Birmingham, in the U.K. It has a very strong industrial past, and that has influenced my work in the past, and still interests me a great deal now. I also lived near a large rural area, so I'd spend a lot of my childhood in the countryside along with my father. I used to collect Wood Elves from the fantasy war game Warhammer. I was pretty young so never really played the game, so I just painted them, and imagined what they'd get up to.

WAS THIS ABOUT THE TIME WHEN YOU FIRST STARTED TO DRAW? Yeah, when I was young, I would draw cartoon characters from television and also make my own comics. I started out with Chip Man, a superhero chip that fought other fast foods. I also drew a lot of DragonBall Z–based comic strips. They were all terrible, but I was dedicated.

DID YOU GO TO ART SCHOOL? I didn't study art at school. At college, I studied English, psychology, and communications studies, but after I'd finished, I forgot all that, enrolled in an art foundation course, and went from there.

WHAT ARE SOME OF THE ADVANTAGES OF WORKING IN BRISTOL? Well, the rent is very cheap, so it makes it affordable to get started as an artist. And especially in the summer, there's a lot going on here, and it's not far from London, which is obviously an important place. Recently, a lot of friends have been moving out, and quite a few are going to London. I did a recent piece entitled HOME that was based on a close friend in particular who left, whom I helped move into London and out of Bristol. I know I'll be doing the same at some point too, so it ended up being a reflection of my thoughts on the whole thing as well.

WHAT ARE SOME OF THESE FOLK TALES AND LEGENDS THAT HAVE INSPIRED YOU? I've recently been reading THE PROSE EDDA, an Icelandic text from around 1220, which explains the origins of a lot of the Norse Mythology. My past work has been influenced by Greek and Native American mythology. Also, Homer's ODYSSEY.

CAN YOU DESCRIBE THE STEPS YOU TAKE TO CREATE AN IMAGE? My work process is very much print-based. I follow all the steps you would if you were to screenprint the image or create a lithograph. The only difference is I use the computer to compose and produce the final imagery instead, both for practical reasons, and because I don't have immediate access to print facilities. I'll draw my imagery in black ink or black pastel or black crayon, and I'll take apart each image to form layers of detail. I then scan in the separations and rather than pull ink through the screen or turn the inked roller, I'll cut them out of a printed texture in Photoshop. I'll layer them up like prints still, but I'm letting the computer do the print side of things. And yes, the graphics tablet and scanner are important to my work, but so is the pot of black ink and my two favorite brushes. It's nice to need so little sometimes. If work crops up, and I'm away from the studio or out of town, it's easy enough to take that stuff with me.

1. _____ **Rest Young Weary One, 2010** Private Commission INK|DIGITAL

2. _____ **Try, Try, Try & Try Again, 2011** Tiny Showcase SCREEN PRINT

3. _____ **Out West, 2010** Personal INK|DIGITAL

WAS THIS PROCESS SOMETHING THAT YOU DEVELOPED OVER TIME? A lot of people work this way, so it's no brainer on my part. We had a print work-shop at university that turned my attention to this way of working, but the main reason I prefer this way is because of how I use color. I usually prefer a limited color palette within work, and working for print, you have certain colors that you work with. I'm not great at painting, and blending colors isn't a strong point, so I tend to avoid it.

YOUR WORK IS OFTEN DESCRIBED AS HAVING AN EXCELLENT GRASP OF "MOOD" OR "ATMOSPHERE." HOW IS THAT ACHIEVED? I gained an understanding of how important it can be to communicate a certain "atmosphere" when I read the Ted Hughes short story THE RAINHORSE. It's heavily image-based, and parallels the protagonist's feelings to the environment around him.
I ended up taking a walk through some fields to try to place myself in the book (so I could illustrate it properly), and I think that helped a great deal. But I think the atmosphere thing has been slightly lost in some of my newer work, and is being replaced by a simpler, more graphical approach. I still aim to add atmosphere within certain pieces, and it's usually to do with anything set outdoors. I love the mythology of the woodlands, and a lot of emotion can be attached to such places.

IS YOUR PROCESS DIFFERENT EVERY TIME OR ARE YOU AT THIS POINT ABLE TO GET IT DOWN TO A HIGHLY-REGULATED FORMULA? It will be slightly different each time, but I pretty much have a formula down for my work now. I have various scans of papers that I use for different images, and this alters how the image looks. I usually use a screen-printed texture and some additional mono-printed textures.

WHAT HAS BEEN THE BIGGEST LEARNING EXPERIENCE SINCE YOU'VE STARTED DOING ANIMATIONS? I couldn't use After Effects or Final Cut at all before working on the animations, so I would have to say those two programs! I also learned a great deal about time management. Animation work is very, very time consuming, as I'm sure will be obvious to many people, but it still manages to catch me off guard each time. Also, don't change where you store your files! It's a nightmare when everything disappears because you've moved a folder!

4. **Bad Times, 2011**
Personal
ARTIST BOOK * INK| DIGITAL

5. **Crowds, 2011**
Personal
ARTIST BOOK * INK| DIGITAL

6. **Good Times, 2011**
Personal
ARTIST BOOK * INK| DIGITAL

7. **Work, 2011**
Personal
ARTIST BOOK * INK| DIGITAL

Shout

—

Alessandro Gottardo
aka Shout creates
visual art projects for
advertising campaigns,
design products, and
publishers on four continents.
His work as been recognized by
several international awards,
including the gold medal from
the Society of Illustrators
in New York.

1. _____ **Crosswalk Man, 2011**
Valerio Millefoglie / EMI
ART DIRECTION: FERDINANDO ARNÔ
HANDDRAWN | DIGITAL

2. _____ **Contigencies, 2011**
First Stop
HANDDRAWN | DIGITAL

3. _____ **The Remains**
of the Lent, 2011
Boston Globe
EDITORIAL | HANDDRAWN | DIGITAL

4. _____ **Untitled, 2011**
MSP Comm
HANDDRAWN | DIGITAL

Emiliano Ponzi

Emiliano Ponzi's lush brushstrokes create contemporary scenes with unique personalities. His painterly style, which pops with color and vitality, has appeared in magazines, advertising, publishing, children's books, posters, newspapers, and exhibitions. The New York Times, Los Angeles Times, Time UK, Washington Post, Newsweek, Businessweek, The Boston Globe, and Le Monde are just some of the clients he works for from his studio in Milan, Italy.

1. **Associations Now Magazine, 2011**
ASAE & The Center for Association Leadership
ART DIRECTION: BETH LOWER
EDITORIAL * HANDDRAWN | DIGITAL

2. **La seconda vita di Francesco d'Assisi, 2010**
Fetrinelli Editore
ART DIRECTION: CRISTIANO GUERRI
BOOK COVER * HANDDRAWN | DIGITAL

3. **Elvis Has Left The Building, 2010**
Valerio Millefoglie / EMI
ART DIRECTION: FERDINANDO ARNÖ
HANDDRAWN | DIGITAL

4. **Summer Reading-Crime Stories, 2010**
Filter Magasinet
ART DIRECTION: OLA CARLSON
EDITORIAL * HANDDRAWN | DIGITAL

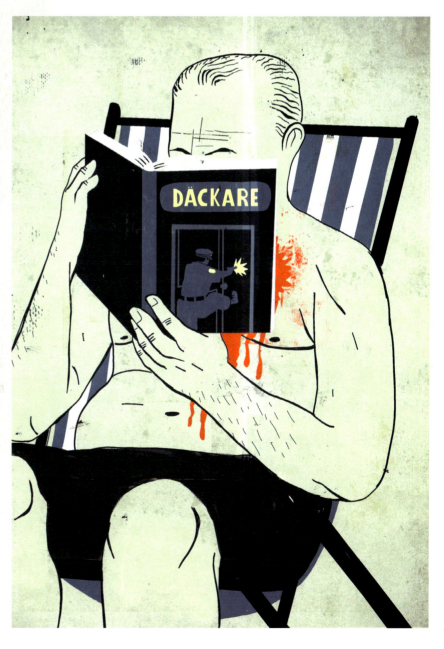

Marc
Smith

Fueled on a diet consisting largely of pasties, flapjacks, and coffee, Mark Smith has built up a worldwide client base including the FINANCIAL TIMES, ESPN MAGAZINE, THE ECONOMIST, The WASHINGTON POST, and THE GUARDIAN. His work has been recognized by 3x3, Society of Illustrators NY, Society of Illustrators LA (bronze medal), CREATIVE QUARTERLY, Association of Illustrators, Creativity International (silver medal), and AMERICAN ILLUSTRATION.

Tavis Coburn

The work of Toronto-based illustrator Tavis Coburn is inspired by 1940s comic book art, the Russian avant-garde movement, and printed materials from the 1950s and '60s. His process, which draws on experience from painting, digital design, and silkscreen, has won him honors from the Society of Publication Designers and the Society of Illustrators, as well as clients in the publishing, advertising, and music business in North America and Europe. He has created motion graphics for Nike, the Los Angeles Chamber of Commerce, and Canadian film and television projects. His advertising and editorial clients include Footlocker, the NFL, TIME, and the DISCOVERY CHANNEL.

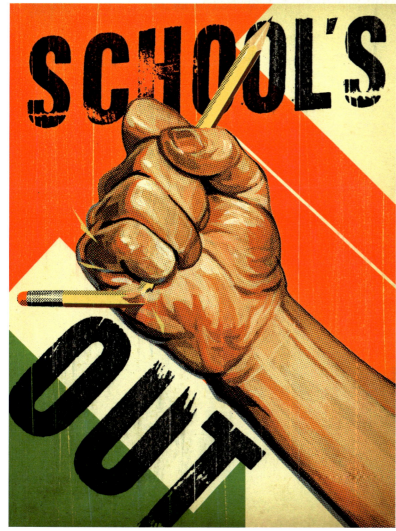

DID ANYTHING IN YOUR HOMETOWN INFLUENCE YOUR STYLE OR CONTENT? I grew up in a suburb of Toronto drawing from comic books and action figures. I started drawing pretty young, and as there were no artists in my family, it seemed very foreign to my parents that I was so absorbed in creating fantastical worlds with pencils and paper. For high school, I attended my district's art school, which was great because we got to double the amount of art classes that a normal high school student would take. I improved a lot over the four years but it paled in comparison to the training I received at Art Center.

YOU CAME RIGHT OUT OF ART CENTER AND STARTED GETTING COMMISSIONS. DID YOU SHOW UP AT SCHOOL WITH YOUR STYLE AND TECHNIQUE PRETTY MUCH IN HAND? OR DID IT DEVELOP OVER YOUR TIME AT SCHOOL? The style I work in today evolved out of some experimentation I was doing at the very end of my time at Art Center. I had taken a lot of courses in printmaking and graphic design while I was there, but my work was still primarily based in painting. One day, I decided to try to separate out a painting into CMYK half tones in order to figure out the nuts and bolts of getting a really good silkscreen print. I still have prints from those first few attempts, and they were a long way from perfect, but they were the roots of what I'm doing today. Once I had that roughly figured out, the rest of the elements of my work started to evolve to work better with that process. My paintings needed to be punchier, with purer colors. Backgrounds needed to be created in ways that would separate out into nice solid colors. And it was all in service of the screenprinting, which was really crucial because it was the process that brought the work together visually in the final product.

WHEN DID YOU MAKE THE SWITCH TO PAINTING IN COREL PAINTER AND USING ILLUSTRATOR, PHOTOSHOP, AND INDESIGN TO PUT THE PIECES TOGETHER? Shortly after I graduated, when I was still in Los Angeles and had a full screenprinting studio of my own, my work was 90 percent handmade and only 10 percent digital. I'd take my reference photos on film. I sat down at a drafting table and painted gouache on paper that mounted to Plexiglas. When a painting was done, it got scanned in, and composited with a background and design elements created in Adobe Illustrator. The finalized image was then printed out of InDesign to my film positive printer and the film was burned to screens. I would frantically try to get as tight a print possible with whatever time I had left. Then I packed up that hopefully perfect print and stuck it in a padded mailer and rushed it over to the local Fed Ex, praying that I made the day's drop-off deadline! When I moved back to Toronto, I realized that I couldn't possibly bring my screenprinting studio with me: drying racks, wash basins, pressure washers, screens—it would have filled a moving truck of its own. So I committed to figuring out how to replicate the look digitally. I settled on a process that used Photoshop's blending modes to create a final digital composite of the film I had always printed, but that would previously have been exposed onto a silkscreen. To this point, the changes in my process were out of necessity, not by choice. But I eventually started thinking of ways I could speed things up, cut out some laborious steps altogether, and save my hands and sanity from the extra work created when clients requested changes. So I started experimenting with 3D modeling, and I started building a library of resources I could reuse. I now use 3D models built in Cinema 4D and ZBrush for comps, which saves a lot of time and gives me a very accurate reference for lighting and proportion. The lone holdout from my old process was that I was still painting in gouache on top of printouts of my 3D model reference, but I eventually decided to invest the time to get comfortable with Corel Painter, which has its own obvious set of benefits over physically painting on paper.

HOW DO YOU GO ABOUT ACHIEVING THAT PULP ATMOSPHERE IN A DIGITAL ENVIRONMENT? IS IT DIFFERENT EVERY TIME OR ARE YOU AT THIS POINT ABLE TO GET IT DOWN TO A HIGHLY REGULATED FORMULA? My process is the same every time except for the rare jobs that have some sort of technical limitations for the artwork. I think my approach to painting, my design sense, and my color choices are very much of the era I'm referencing, so even if I have to abandon the halftones for a job, it can still be injected with the same aesthetic.

ARE THERE ANY SPECIFIC PULP GRAPHICS FROM THE 1940 AND 1950S THAT WERE ESPECIALLY MEMORABLE? I have an extensive library of old pulp magazines and books from that era, as well as contemporary books that collect work from those periods. To narrow my influences down to even a handful of names would be difficult. I don't tend to look to one particular artist for inspiration, or to see how they solved a particular visual problem. But I won't hesitate to search through a few years' worth of POPULAR SCIENCE magazines from the 1960s to see if an illustrator who I'd never heard of might have a brilliant way of creating a specific effect. I do, however, flip through the work of Gil Elvgren and Robert McGinnis every single time I'm faced with painting a woman.

1. **The Hurt Locker, 2010**
British Academy of Film
and Television Arts
ART DIRECTOR: GUY MARSHALL/
AGENCY: STUDIO SMALL
EVENT PROGRAM COVER * DIGITAL

2. **Beltran, 2008**
American Express
ART DIRECTOR: PATRICIA LOCKE
BOOK * DIGITAL

3. **Back To School, 2008**
Canadian Business
ART DIRECTOR: BETH LOWER
EDITORIAL * DIGITAL

Paul Blow

Paul Blow's favorite color is accountant blue. His most treasured possessions are his glasses, which are with him at all times. The words he lives by are: blood, sweat, and tears. He can be found staring at blank paper with bleeding eyes from his studio somewhere in the U.K.

His work can be found in the BOSTON GLOBE, the TIMES, and every two weeks on the GUARDIAN's comments page along with the work of writer and broadcaster Simon Jenkins.

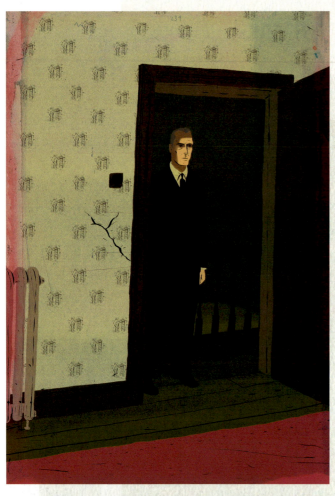

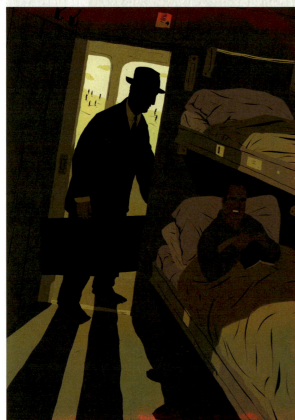

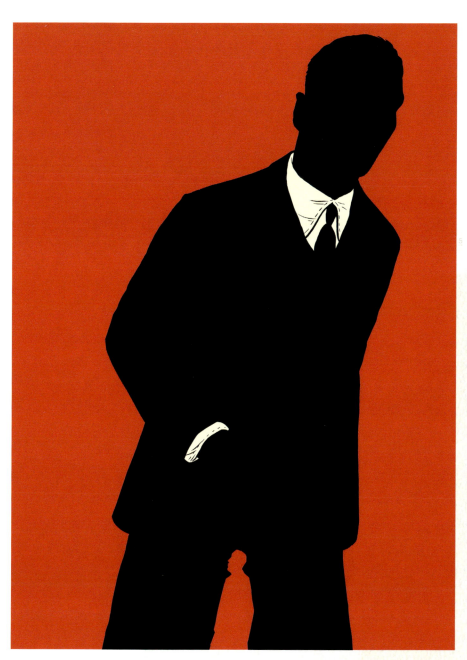

1.|2.|3.|5.|6. **Mask of Dimitrios, 2011**
Folio Society
BOOK * MIXED MEDIA

4. **iPad, 2010**
The Guardian
EDITORIAL * MIXED MEDIA

7. **Tiger Feet, 2011**
The Guardian
EDITORIAL * MIXED MEDIA

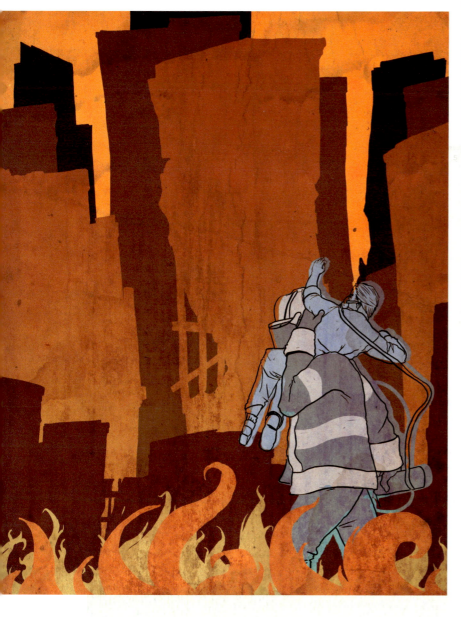

Michael Hirshon

After a nomadic childhood spent doodling, eating, sleeping, and growing, Michael Hirshon ended up in St. Louis, USA, where he studied illustration and design. His work, which uses simple line work and color palettes, has been honored by a number of institutions including the Society of Illustrators and the AIGA. He counts American Express, the LOS ANGELES TIMES, and the OC WEEKLY amongst his many clients.

1. **Skateboardin' Gramps, 2010**
Personal
PRINT * HAND DRAWN | DIGITAL

2. **Soccer Riot, 2009**
Personal
PRINT * HAND DRAWN | DIGITAL

3. **The Bugs, 2010**
Personal
BOOK * HAND DRAWN | DIGITAL

4. **Losing It, 2010**
St. Louis Magazine
ART DIRECTOR: KEVIN GOODBAR,
TEXT: JEANNETTE COOPERMAN
EDITORIAL * HAND DRAWN | DIGITAL

5. **Horace in the Big City, 2009**
Personal
BOOK * HAND DRAWN | DIGITAL

6. **St. Louis Decal, 2010**
American Express
ART DIRECTOR: TOM GRILLO
WINDOW DECAL * HAND DRAWN | DIGITAL

7. **Rasputin: Salvation after Sin, 2010**
Personal
EDITORIAL * HAND DRAWN | DIGITAL

8. **Cartilage Damage, 2009**
Personal
EDITORIAL * HAND DRAWN | DIGITAL

Peter Diamond

Peter Diamond was raised in Canada, where he went to art school and discovered artists such as Yuko Shimizu, Chris Buzelli, Marcos Chin, Jeff Domm, and Mike Mesheau, who would all have a great influence on his work. His highly detailed and richly colored illustrations have been used by the NEW YORK TIMES, Roadrunner Records, and the World Wildlife Fund, and recognized by AMERICAN ILLUSTRATION, the Society of Illustrators, and 3 x 3. Diamond lives in Vienna, Austria, where he also writes and teaches drawing workshops.

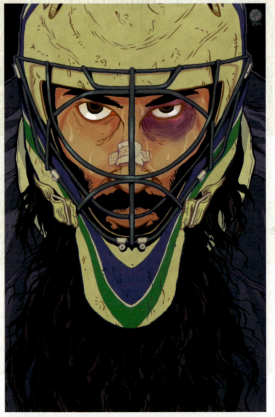

Patrick Leger

The retro-style illustrations of North Carolina-based illustrator Patrick Leger have been featured in many publications including the WASHINGTON POST, THE NEW YORKER, and WIRED UK. His drawings are colorful and high-contrast, clearly revealing the vintage comics and illustrations that have influenced his work.

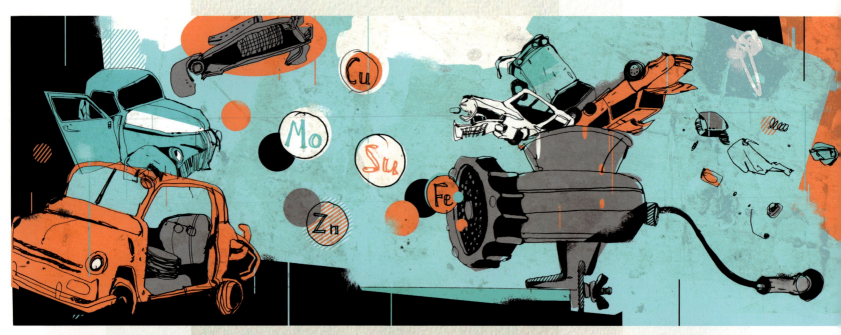

1. **Junk, 2007**
AutoNews Magazine
EDITORIAL * MIXED MEDIA

2. **Sex, 2007**
GQ Magazine
EDITORIAL * MIXED MEDIA

3. **Werewolf, 2009**
Men's Health Magazine
EDITORIAL * MIXED MEDIA

4. **Toreador, 2007**
Russian Digital Magazine
ART DIRECTOR: NIKOLAY GLADUSHEV
EDITORIAL * MIXED MEDIA

Valentin Tkach

Valentin Tkach lives and works in Moscow, creating illustrations for GQ, MEN'S HEALTH, and ROLLING STONE, amongst others.

5 **Divorce, 2008**
GQ Magazine
ILLUSTRATION * MIXED MEDIA

6 **Glass, 2011**
Noon, Twenty-First Century Magazine
ART DIRECTOR: ANTON FEDOROV
EDITORIAL * MIXED MEDIA

7 **New Moscow, 2010**
Snob.ru
ART DIRECTOR: IGOR BURMAKIN
EDITORIAL * MIXED MEDIA

8 **Tourist, 2010**
Russian Newsweek
ART DIRECTOR: ALEXANDER BYLOV
EDITORIAL * MIXED MEDIA

Pietari Posti

1. _____ **No Sex, 2008**
Olivia Magazine
EDITORIAL * DIGITAL

2. _____ **Finland, 2008**
National Geographic
Adventure
EDITORIAL * MIXED DIGITAL

3. ____ **Lost in the Sea of Love, 2009**
Annabelle Magazine
EDITORIAL * MIXED DIGITAL

4. _____ **Untitled, 2010**
Personal
EDITORIAL * DIGITAL

5. _____ **Saigon, 2010**
United Airlines
EDITORIAL * DIGITAL

Pietari Posti is a Finnish freelance illustrator living and working in Barcelona, Spain. His work is a combination of mixed media and digital, though he prefers to work by hand to create images that are inspired by the visual culture of art, graphic design, comics, and packaging that surround him in his adopted country. Justin Wood, Mr. Ed, Klaus Haapaniemi, Tim Biskup, and Mike Giant are several of the illustrators whose work he particularly admires. His work has appeared in the New York Times, Wired, and on T-shirts, advertisements, and book covers. Pietari's work has been featured in the 3x3 Professional Illustration Annual, PRINT Magazine European Design Annual, and American Illustration 27 and 28.

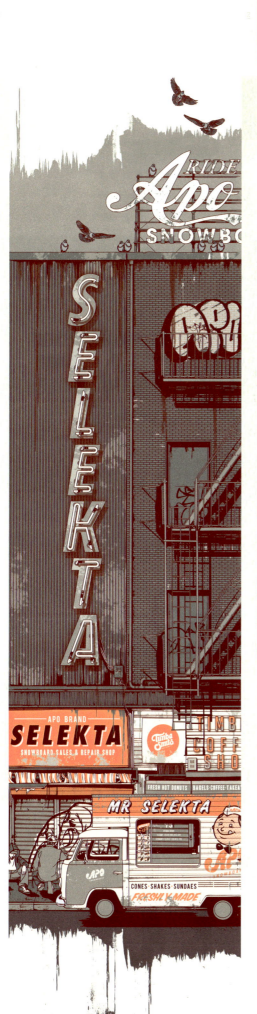

Timba Smits

1,2 _____ **Selekta, 2011**
APO Snowboards France
SNOWBOARD GRAPHIC • DIGITAL

3 _____ **Street / Studio, 2010**
Thames & Hudson
BOOK COVER • DIGITAL

Timba Smits is an award-winning graphic designer, artist, illustrator, independent publisher, self-confessed magazine addict, and wanna-be Olympic ping-pong player with a proper love of all things retro and kitsch. He is also founder of WOODEN TOY QUARTERLY, the half book, half zine about culture, design, and art. It is advertising from the 1940s to the 1960s that permeates his illustration work, as well as an assortment of other influences such as the pin-up artists artists George Petty and Gil Elvgren and newer discoveries like Gary Taxali, CandyKiller, Mike Giant, and Tyler Stout. Timba Smits was born in Melbourne, Australia, and is based in London, UK.

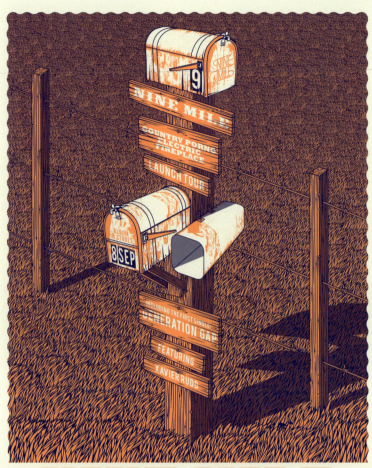

Matthew Woodson

Matthew Woodson grew up in southern Indiana in a house hidden away in a ravine in the woods, and these natural surroundings of his childhood have followed him and his work, appearing as a background for the characters who populate his work. But he is also heavily influenced by older movies, such as those by director John Ford, vintage art and design, and especially pre-war blues and folk, with "all the grittiness and Old Testament emotions just bubbling away beneath the surface," he says.

His narrative style, which takes its cues from classic comic book art, has been used by clients such as the Boston Globe, ESPN, Perry Ellis, and Spin magazine. He currently lives and works in Chicago.

1. **Untitled, 2007**
UNICEF
ART DIRECTOR: DREW CROWLEY
HAND DRAWN | DIGITAL

2. **Red Robin, 2011**
Personal
HAND DRAWN | DIGITAL

3. **Rest Assured, 2011**
Personal
HAND DRAWN | DIGITAL

WHEN DID YOU FIRST START TO DRAW? There is no real way for me to pinpoint exactly when I started drawing, though I do clearly remember drawing a character named "Melf the Elf" that my father had invented as a bedtime story. I don't remember much about him other than the fact that he wore an acorn top as a hat and had a boat made of leaves. I must have been four or five.

DID YOUR HOMETOWN INFLUENCE YOUR INTEREST IN NATURAL HISTORY? Growing up in the middle of the woods definitely still echoes in my work even today. I spent the majority of my childhood exploring, digging in the dirt, or trying to catch frogs in our pond. I grew to love the aesthetics of nature, the contradictions of both simplicity and complexity that are in natural forms. Natural history illustration and taxidermy just seemed like a natural step.

WOULD YOU SAY THEN THAT YOU ARE LARGELY SELF-TAUGHT? It's hard to say—there was definitely no one who taught me to draw, but I had a lot of support from my family. My father was good with music and carpentry, and my grandmother was a draftswoman. She would send me art tutorial books she found at estate sales. I coveted them—they were massively helpful even though I can't say they were exactly appropriate for my age … I don't know many seven-year-olds who were teaching themselves three-point perspective from books aimed towards architecture students printed in the early 1960s.

CAN YOU DESCRIBE THE STEPS YOU TAKE TO CREATE AN IMAGE? It's pretty simple. I do all of my line work with ink on paper, usually with brush and quill, but sometimes with ruling pens and other archaic drawing tools, a lot of which are from my grandmother's drafting arsenal. I then scan the images into my computer and apply colors and effects with programs like Photoshop and Illustrator. I also use a lot of textures and antiqued paper in "post production" on my pieces that I have collected over the years. I have yet to decide if using a computer in my work is either a curse or a godsend.

SO IS THE PROCESS DIFFERENT EVERY TIME OR ARE YOU AT THIS POINT ABLE TO GET IT DOWN TO A HIGHLY REGULATED FORMULA? I try to avoid a regulated formula because I end up using some processes or techniques as a crutch, which ultimately leads to dull work … and more importantly, to me being bored with what I am doing. I try to switch things around a lot. The more unconventionally I approach a piece, the more interesting the final outcome is.

SO DID YOU SHOW UP AT SCHOOL WITH YOUR STYLE AND TECHNIQUE PRETTY MUCH IN HAND? OR DID IT DEVELOP DURING YOUR TIME THERE? I have been known to say on several occasions that I did not learn anything from art school, which is only partly true. I came into school knowing exactly what I wanted to do, and how I wanted to do it. I was already equipped with the majority of the technical skills I still use today, but what art school did teach me was how to handle my concepts with more subtlety, which really forced me to mature as an artist.

WHAT WAS SO INFLUENTIAL ABOUT PEOPLE LIKE BRIAN WOOD AND ADRIAN TOMINE? I have been referencing Brian Wood and Adrian Tomine a lot recently since I have gotten back into comics and graphic novels. When I was in high school, both Wood and Tomine were doing comics the way I wanted to do comics. It wasn't all about glitz and glamour, huge-breasted women and men with oversized guns … they were doing comics about people and emotions, things I could relate to. They were using comics as a vehicle to tell a story, or as I have called it in the past, "drawing movies."

WHAT OR WHO WERE SOME OF YOUR OTHER INFLUENCES? My list of inspirations is terribly long. Recently, I have been looking at a lot of mid-century artists and illustrators like Franklin Arbuckle, Bernard D'Andrea, Joe Bowler, Jon Whitcomb, Andy Virgil, the list goes on and on. Their ability to tell complex stories in a single image makes me light-headed to think about. I also really enjoy Renaissance art (Raphael's under-drawings blew my mind in college), Greek sculpture, and religious artwork—heavy emotion and symbology, I don't think that needs much explaining. And of course I cannot talk about inspiration with out mentioning John James Audubon. He had a way of depicting animals that felt like a person had not actually painted what was there on the paper. It's as if the animals actually exist there in the artwork.

1 | 2 . 13. **Untitled, 2011**
Annabelle Magazine
ART DIRECTOR: KELLER ANNETTE
EDITORIAL * HAND DRAWN | DIGITAL

4 **Untitled, 2011**
New York Magazine
ART DIRECTOR: RAUL AGUILA
EDITORIAL * HAND DRAWN | DIGITAL

5 **Untitled, 2009**
Puma
ADVERTISING * HAND DRAWN | DIGITAL

WHAT IS IT ABOUT ANATOMY AND NATURAL HISTORY THAT YOU FIND SO COMPELLING AS A SUBJECT? Referencing anatomical and natural history art in my work allows me to humanize and personify concepts that can be too easily force-fed to a viewer by drawing people. It allows me to show things that people may have never paid attention to before, and in turn that makes the work more compelling. This is another access point for me to challenge myself in my own work. And on a more personal note, nature is what has always come—for lack of a better term—naturally to me. Depicting natural elements allows me to show things like frailty, longing, strength, and passion in ways that nothing else really can.

SO WHAT IS YOUR HANDS-DOWN FAVORITE THING TO DRAW? If I had to pick one, it would be glasses, especially if they are being worn. Not only are the angles, distortions of the eyes beneath, and reflections a real challenge to draw; there is something about getting it all drawn correctly that is so extremely satisfying. I really enjoy drawing things that are simple to draw, but hard to draw well, things like glasses, hair, and hands.

Adam Devarney

Adam DeVarney's work investigates the layering of ideas; he combines drawings and acrylic wash with found images and other paper media on wood panel. His work is disparate in content, which creates a dream-like history when juxtaposed. Skateboarding art, urban contemporary art, vintage illustration, comics, and cartoons as well as urban culture, popular culture, design, music, and old movies are just some of the things he draws inspiration from. He lives and works in Burlington, USA, where he was born and raised.

1. **Pennsylvania Six Five Thousand, 2010**
Personal
PAINTING * DRAWING|MIXED MEDIA

2. **Citizen's Broadband Radio, 2010**
Personal
PAINTING * DRAWING|MIXED MEDIA

3. **Major Appliance, 2010**
Personal
PAINTING * DRAWING|MIXED MEDIA

4. **High Temperature Cutoff, 2011**
Personal
PAINTING * DRAWING|MIXED MEDIA

5. **Three Blind Mice (Red), 2011**
Personal
PAINTING * DRAWING|MIXED MEDIA

6. **Man at High Altitude, 2010**
Personal
PAINTING * DRAWING|MIXED MEDIA

7. **Atlas At Last, 2011**
Personal
PAINTING * DRAWING|MIXED MEDIA

8. **Flashpoint, 2010**
Personal
PAINTING * DRAWING|MIXED MEDIA

Yuko Shimizu

Yuko Shimizu creates her work at the intersection of traditional Japanese graphic prints and surreal comic art. The award-winning New York-based artist draws her basic forms and figures with calligraphy brushes before digitally supplementing them with additional colors and backgrounds. This technique results in elegant and harmoniously composed creative visions and science-fiction fantasies, which are often erotically charged and combine the best of American pop and Japanese comic culture.

3×3

現代イラスト誌 三掛三

1_____**Baku, 2008**
Fantagraphics Books
ART DIRECTOR: JACOB COVEY
BOOK * DRAWING | MIXED MEDIA

2_____**Chasers, 2008**
Plansponsor Magazine
ART DIRECTOR: SOOJIN BUZELLI
EDITORIAL * DRAWING | MIXED MEDIA

3_____**Risking for more, 2008**
Planadvisor Magazine
ART DIRECTOR: MAYNARD KAY
EDITORIAL * DRAWING | MIXED MEDIA

4_____**Frogfolio, 2007**
Dellas Graphics
ART DIRECTOR: JIM BURKE
CALENDAR * DRAWING | MIXED MEDIA

Sean Lewis

Toronto-based illustrator Sean Lewis's most recent work is a series of painterly portraits based on outlaws such as Pablo Escobar, Ed Gein, and the Unabomber. The Black Bart and George Gordon portraits received a gold from 3x3, a magazine of contemporary illustration.

1. **Ed Gein, 2011**
   OCADU
   CREDIT: PAUL DALLAS
   THESIS * ACRYLIC

2. **Unabomber, 2011**
   OCADU
   CREDIT: PAUL DALLAS
   THESIS * ACRYLIC

3. **Vine, 2009**
   Personal
   PAINTING * ACRYLIC

4. **Canoe, 2009**
   Personal
   PAINTING * ACRYLIC|PEN

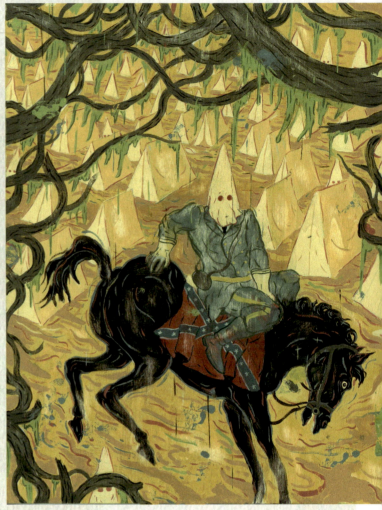

1. ___ **Never Too Perfect, 2009**
OCADU
CREDIT: PAUL DALLAS
THESIS * ACRYLIC

2. ___ **George Gordon, 2011**
OCADU
CREDIT: PAUL DALLAS
THESIS * ACRYLIC

3. ___ **John Torrio, 2011**
OCADU
CREDIT: PAUL DALLAS
THESIS * ACRYLIC

4. ___ **Pablo Escobar, 2011**
OCADU
CREDIT: PAUL DALLAS
THESIS * ACRYLIC

5. ___ **Sea, 2009**
Personal
PAINTING * ACRYLIC

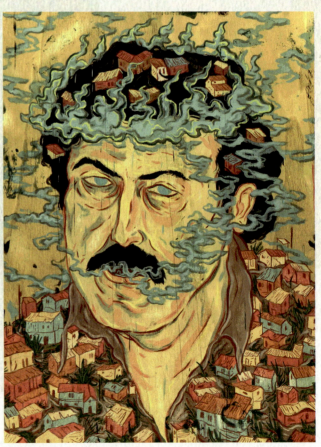

Andres Guzman

Born in Lima, Peru, Andres Guzman moved to Denver, USA, when he was a child. His working style is diverse, giving away his love of various working processes and influences; one sees pop art, comic book art, and realism in his illustrations. His work has been published in THRASHER MAGAZINE, THE WEEKLY DIG, CREATIVE QUARTERLY 15, CMYK MAGAZINE, COLOR MAGAZINE, and the WASHINGTON SQUARE REVIEW. His clients include Nickelodeon, MTV, VICE MAGAZINE, and Rhymesayers Entertainment.

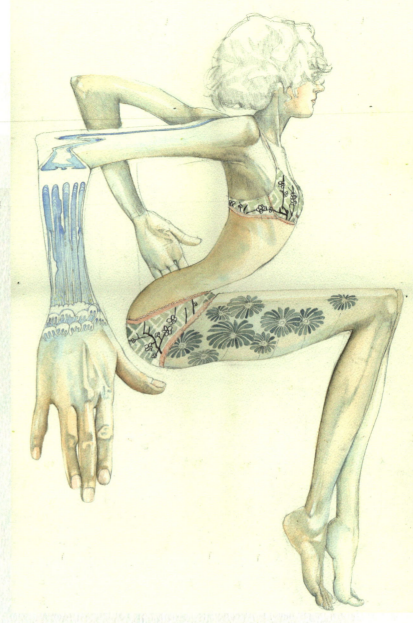

Daniel Mackie

In 2010, illustrator Daniel Mackie abandoned Photoshop and became an illustrator who works exclusively with watercolor. His illustrations, which are created on heavy 300gsm paper, have been used in editorial, publishing, design, and advertising projects for clients such as Adobe, BP, British Airways, the ECONOMIST, ESQUIRE, the FINANCIAL TIMES, GQ, The GUARDIAN, Penguin, Random House, and Virgin. He lives and works in London, U.K.

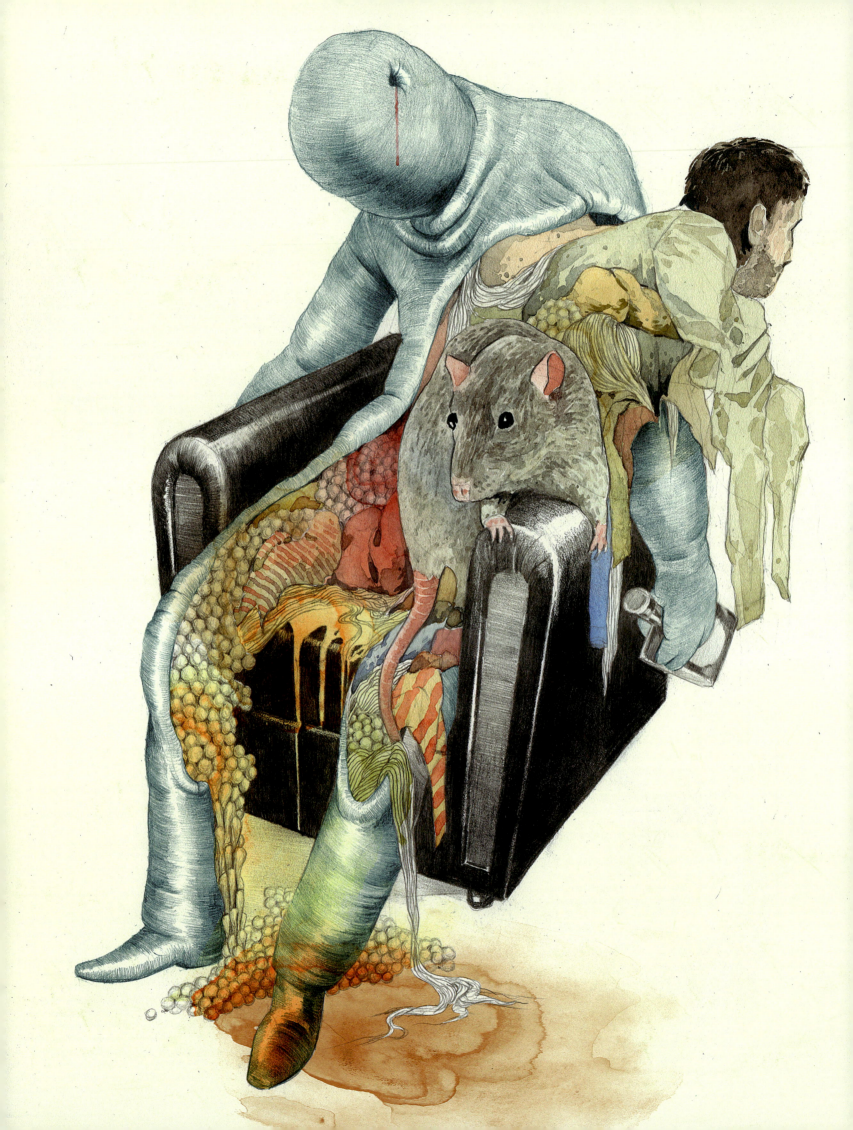

Dmitry Ligay

1–4 **Cold, 2010**
Snob Magazine
ART DIRECTOR: ILYA BARANOV,
DESIGNER: ALEXANDRA KUZNETSOVA
EDITORIAL ON ANDREY GELASIMOV ·
MIXED MEDIA

The work of
Dmitry Ligay,
who was born
in Tashkent,
Uzbekistan,
has a classic, handmade feeling to it,
evoking a time long before the advent
of digitally produced illustration.
Although an architecture student
at the beginning of his studies,
he switched to the illustration
department, where he began to
develop his often figurative work.
His clients include Russian
advertising agencies, and
magazines.

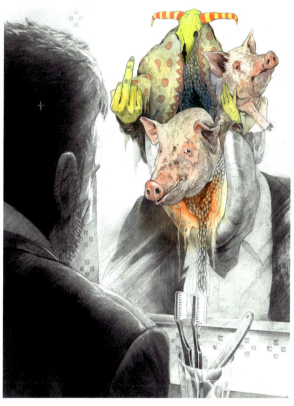

Caitlin Hackett

The relationship between humans and animals is the predominant theme in Caitlin Hackett's work. Raised in Arcata, California, near the famed Redwood National Park, her hand-drawn images, often rendered in ballpoint pen and watercolor, take their cue from the symbolic treatment of animals in mythology, religious imagery, and cultural dialogues. She alludes to the boundaries that separate humans from animals—and how the objectification and personification of animals alters these boundaries. Currently, Hackett lives and works in Brooklyn, New York, where she also works as a creature designer for a video game company. In October, her work will be included in the exhibition "Breath of Embers: Art of Dragons," at Nucleus Gallery in Los Angeles. She is also included in the group show "Dark Waters," curated by Martin Wittfooth at CoproGallery in Santa Monica, opening in November.

WHAT WAS IT THAT INSPIRED YOU TO BEGIN DRAWING? I've been drawing for as long as I can remember. My parents would set down a stack of printer paper, no sketchbooks, and a bucket of every conceivable crayon, and my twin sister and I would literally sit there for hours, and draw and narrate stories to go with the pictures. And they were all animals. No people. Cats with wings and unicorns and horses, and there was never just one, there were tons of them on a page. As kids, our parents would take us camping, and so we were introduced to the natural world at a very young age, especially because my dad was very interested in it.

WAS YOUR DAD THE TYPE OF GUY WHO KNEW THE NAMES OF ALL THE TREES? Oh yeah, he had every conceivable book on birds of North America, wildflowers of North America. We'd go up to Horse Mountain and he'd point out madrones, aspens, blue firs. And in the summer, it's like a desert with all these bone-dry, white trees. It's the most alien landscape—there's this volcanic soil, so the trees are all stunted. A lot of the trees I draw are probably based on those because they're all mostly skeletal, sculptural trees. And you don't get those really leafy trees there—the redwoods' branches start so high up and they're so tall, it's like being in a cathedral.

SO WOULD YOU CONSIDER YOURSELF SELF-TAUGHT? I was definitely drawing before I went to school and was definitely drawing animals, but going to Pratt influenced my style mostly because it forced me to draw from life for awhile. Most of my things come from my head but I've learned that to really study a texture you have to spend some time looking at it.

HOW WOULD YOU SAY YOUR STYLE OR TECHNIQUE EVOLVED OVER YOUR TIME AT SCHOOL? My sophomore year I had a great professor, one of the rare ones who was really supportive but wouldn't let you bullshit your way through the class. I hadn't yet discovered you could buy giant rolls of paper so my work was still really small. And at the same time, I had a different professor who was actually a sculptor—I don't know why she was teaching a drawing class—but I am convinced that she loathes two-dimensional objects. I was advised by multiple people to go into the illustration department instead of the fine art department, which is a distinction I find to be ridiculous. But anyway, every week I just started bringing in my work and making it bigger and bigger, like, if it's larger, is it still illustration?

WHO ELSE WOULD YOU SAY INFLUENCED YOU? When I started, I would also cut my pieces out and put them in installations. I had seen some of the work of Hannah Docherty, who's an artist who does these scientific illustration animals, but cuts them out and puts them on wood, and combines sculpture and drawing in a way that I find fascinating. I like this idea of multimedia where drawing, painting and illustration don't have to be so rigidly defined.

SO YOU LIKED THE DRAWINGS BIGGER? Now I have a hard time composing small pieces, I end up going outside the page, like I can't contain the seams. There's also something about it being life-size, as if it feels more real. I saw a show of Walton Ford [at the Brooklyn Museum] and thought, wow, this guy is amazing, who cares about still lifes or what medium I'm working in?

DO YOU FIND FACES HARD TO DRAW? People always say noses are hardest but I think the mouth is the hardest because that's where you show your character. All mouths are different. Noses are hard, yeah, but they have the same basic structure. With mouths, you have smile lines or frown lines, and that is what I still have trouble with. But I need that human structure in my drawings, and you need it to be right. With animals, people may not even really know if it's done correctly, but with the human parts, we all know what a hand or an arm should look like, and how it should function.

DOES THAT HUMAN ELEMENT MAKE YOUR ANIMALS MORE REALISTIC AS WELL? Yeah, I think it also helps people relate to them. One of the things I'm interested in is how a human body could be an animal body—what would you have to do to make your arm look like a wing? Or how would you fold your body into that position? Because technically, we are a species of animal. We spend so much time in our heads that you can forget that you have this huge clumsy body that you're loafing around, and have this bizarre bone structure. Animals have to live within their physical means and they are always present inside their bodies. They don't have the luxury of designing art or going online and checking Facebook. We live a lot in our mental space.

WHAT IS YOUR FAVORITE THING TO DRAW? Birds, probably, and foxes. As a kid, it was all horses and cats but if I'm stumped, I'll start sketching and it almost always turns out to be birds. There's something very cool about the eyes of a bird and the different kind of beaks. I especially love the Cassowary bird or turkey, anything with waddles or weird wrinkles. I love every kind of vulture.

Yuta Onoda

The illustrator and painter Yuta Onoda, originally from Japan, is now based in Toronto, Canada. His favorite drawing tools are pencils, ballpoint pens and brush pens, acrylic paint, and colored pencils, which he combines with digital techniques to create images for magazines and publishers including Simon & Schuster and the ATLANTIC.

1.   **Itinerant Killer, 2010**
West Magazine
ART DIRECTOR: TERESA JOHNSTON
EDITORIAL * MIXED MEDIA | DIGITAL

2.   **I As Nature, 2009**
Earth Island Journal
Magazine
MANAGING EDITOR: AMY WESTERVELT
EDITORIAL * MIXED MEDIA | DIGITAL

3.   **To Lost Friends
and Fallen Comrades, 2009**
Modern Dog Magazine
CREATIVE DIRECTOR: JENNIFER NOSEK
EDITORIAL * MIXED MEDIA | DIGITAL

4.   **Please Me
One More Time, 2009**
Personal
POSTER * MIXED MEDIA | DIGITAL

5.   **Exploring the Void, 2010**
Popular Mechanics
ART DIRECTOR: PETER HERBERT
EDITORIAL * MIXED MEDIA | DIGITAL

Thomas Kuhlenbeck

Illustrator Thomas Kuhlenbeck divides his work into two styles: realistic and outline. Within each style he works with a number of contemporary themes including economy, politics, technology and lifestyle. DER SPIEGEL, THE WALLSTREET JOURNAL, TIME magazine, FORBES, and DIE ZEIT are just some of his many clients.

1. **Fashion Twins, 2011**
The Wall Street Journal
ART DIRECTOR: MARK TYNER
EDITORIAL • HAND DRAWN |
ACRYLICS | DIGITAL

2. **David Bowie, 2010**
Personal
PAINTING • HAND DRAWN |
ACRYLICS | DIGITAL

3. **Fresno 8, 2011**
Förderverein Aktuelle
Kunst Münster e.V.
POSTER • HAND DRAWN |
ACRYLICS | DIGITAL

4. **Wasser, 2011**
FB 69 Gallery
CALENDAR PRINT • HAND DRAWN |
ACRYLICS | DIGITAL

5. **Der Rauch, 2011**
Personal
PAINTING • HAND DRAWN | ACRYLICS

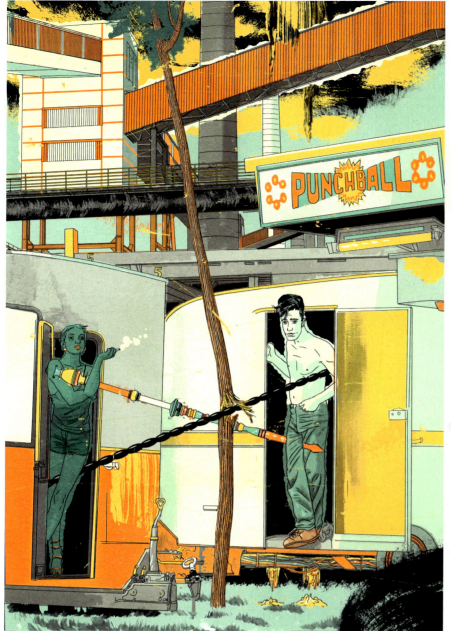

Byron Eggenschwiler

Browsing through Byron Eggenschwiler's portfolio reveals a world of people and animals who are often involved in curious situations. This stems, he explains, from an interest in never knowing how a human/animal encounter will end up, and narratives that do not necessarily draw up a neat conclusion, or present their intentions too obviously. The Calgary-based illustrator's work has been featured in many publications including the WALL STREET JOURNAL, the NEW YORK TIMES, and the LA WEEKLY and recognized at the prestigious 2011 Society of Illustrators Awards. His portrait of William Shatner was included in THE SHATNER SHOW book. Unless working on a Personal he uses a Wacom tablet, Digital, and his MacbookPro.

1. **Why Wait for Fate?, 2010**
National Post
DESIGN EDITOR: DANIEL DESOUZA
HOROSKOPE – EDITORIAL * INK | DIGITAL

2._____ **Harmful Chemicals Found in School Supplies, 2009**
SEE magazine
ART DIRECTOR: MICHAEL NUNWEILER
COVER * INK | DIGITAL

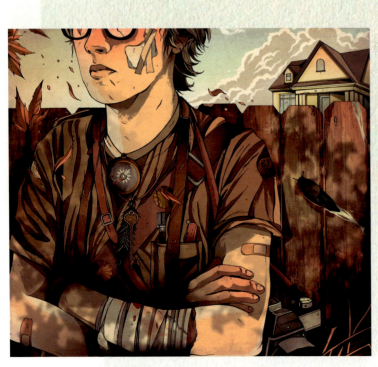

Alexander Wells

Alexander Wells is a freelance illustrator living in Brighton, U.K. He creates images with both traditional and digital techniques for clients including Glenfiddich whiskey, WIRED magazine, the GUARDIAN, MOJO magazine, and the FINANCIAL TIMES.

1   **Tiger in the Long Grass, 2011**
Personal
HAND DRAWN | DIGITAL

2   **The Suburban Adventure, 2011**
Personal
HAND DRAWN | DIGITAL

3   **The Catcher in the Rye, 2010**
Personal
HAND DRAWN | DIGITAL

4   **Pin Me Up, 2011**
Personal
HAND DRAWN | DIGITAL

5   **Two, 2011**
Personal
HAND DRAWN | DIGITAL

6   **Frog Soup, 2010**
Personal
HAND DRAWN | DIGITAL

7   **Tobe Hooper, 2011**
Wired (US)
ART DIRECTOR: ALICE CHO
EDITORIAL * HAND DRAWN | DIGITAL

Victo Ngai

Before moving to the United States for her education, Victo Ngai lived in Hong Kong, where she was born and raised. She now lives and works in New York City, producing work that reveals a love of Japanese wood-block prints. Her work is executed both traditionally and digitally; lines are drawn with pens, while paper, graphite, acrylic, oil, and pastels help her achieve various textures. But all of it is digitally composed and colored with Photoshop. Her published work includes illustrations for Plansponsor and Deal magazines as well as the New York Times op-ed page. Her work has been featured in 3x3, Communication Arts Illustration Annual, American Illustration Annual, SPECTRUM, Society of Illustrators NY and LA, and CMYK Magazine.

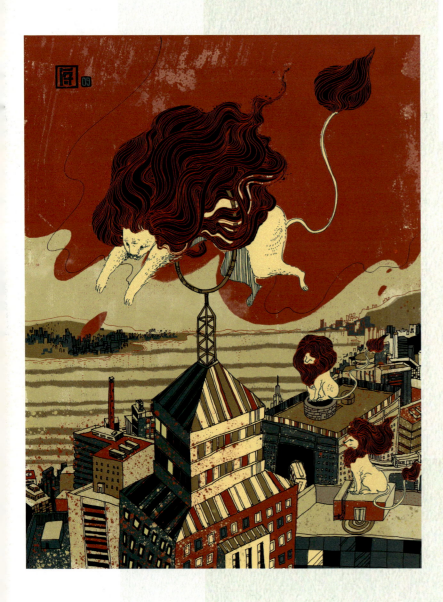

WERE THERE ANY STORIES THAT ATTRACTED YOU WHEN YOU FIRST STARTED TO DRAW? I started drawing and doodling when I was around five. My dad was in the logistics industry and was always out of town; my mom was a newspaper editor and had crazy hours. We couldn't afford a nanny, so my mom would bring me to work, and let me sit at an empty office desk. The only "toys" around were paper and pens so I started drawing out stories to entertain myself, which were mainly half-fabricated, half-Frankensteined from the picture books I read, cartoons I watched, and things that happened in school. I have always been attracted to fantasy and mythological stories, and Tom & Jerry.

SO WOULD YOU SAY THAT YOU LARGELY SELF-TAUGHT? I took after-school art classes on and off as a kid, and two years of art lessons in high school, but didn't have much formal training until I went to Rhode Island School of Design.

DID YOUR EARLY EXPOSURE TO A LOT OF DIFFERENT CULTURES INFLUENCE YOUR WORK? Yeah, I think the mixture of different cultures contributed to my style and my way of thinking. In the U.S., I was often told that my style was very reminiscent of traditional oriental arts and folk crafts. However, in China, people think my works look very Western. If anything, growing up in Hong Kong, a former British colony and an international city where the East and West are woven together seamlessly, provided the early soil that cultivated my works.

WHEN YOU BEGIN TO DEVELOP YOUR STYLE? DID YOU SHOW UP AT SCHOOL WITH IT FULLY FORMED OR HOW MUCH DID IT EVOLVE OVER TIME? To me, RISD is one of those places that if you can make it there, you can make it anywhere, as the saying goes. To say that the classes were intense would be an understatement. For the longest time, I could get no more than four hours of sleep every night, and the school really challenged my limits and pushed my potential in every way. I loved everything about it though (well, maybe not the dark circles around my eyes) but don't think I could do it again. For a while, I was struggling to find "a style" by looking at established illustrators' works, because I thought that was how illustration was "supposed to look." But one of my professors, Chris Buzelli, pointed out that "style is merely one's habit of drawing. Everyone is born with a unique style as everyone is born unique." It helped me find my own honest voice.

WHEN DID YOU COME UP WITH YOUR HALF-TRADITIONAL, HALF-DIGITAL PROCESS? I came up with it when I was at RISD. I love line drawings and flat colors, and I also did a lot of linocuts when I was young, so I tried to find a process that could bring these elements to my illustrations. I usually start drawing with nib pens, sometimes brushes or rapidograph pens, then create layers of textures on separated pieces of paper with various media (pencil, charcoal, crayon, paint) on a lightbox. Afterwards, I have everything scanned, digitally colored, and composed in Photoshop.

IS THIS PROCESS SOMETHING THAT YOU DEVELOPED OVER TIME? My process keeps evolving. In the beginning, I was just trying to find a faster and more flexible alternative to printmaking. Then I started to experiment with different media and methods, and was delightfully surprised by the chemical reactions. I like my works to take on their own lives and surprise me.

ONE THING YOUR IMAGES SEEM TO ALWAYS HAVE ARE VERY CLEAR AND COMMUNICATED CONCEPTS. HOW DO YOU GO ABOUT IDENTIFYING THEM? I always want to get better at coming up with concepts and trying to figure out the best approaches or formula—if there is one. When I start with an assignment, I read through the material a number of times to understand the main point, underlining phrases that give me hunches or jot down words that conjure up images while I'm reading. After I feel like I have a good understanding, I like to stay away from the given material and work with the hunches and elements I extracted—this helps free my thoughts from literal clichés—a businessman with a suitcase, dollar signs, piggy banks, those sorts of things. I would explore and develop these hunches until I get stories, scenarios, or metaphors that work for the main point. Sometimes it helps to think backward too, especially for more abstract concepts. I think of what kind of imageries, color, or design I want to create and try to make that work with the story, which makes the piece that much more personal and fun. The best ideas usually take some luck, and you can never tell where they come from, so it's important to be exposed to as many things as possible and build a large visual language database. Usually, the time I spend on an image is about half of the time on the idea, and half on the execution. Sometimes the idea takes longer, because I want to make sure I am excited enough about what I am going to draw.

WHAT HAS BEEN THE BIGGEST THING YOU'VE LEARNED (OR BIGGEST FRUSTRATION) FROM DOING ANIMATIONS? The biggest thing I have learned is that good drawers are not necessarily good animators. I can make the individual frame look good but good animations are more about timing, pacing, camera movement, motion distortion, and exaggeration. I have seen some animator friends' frame drawings that are pretty sketchy and frankly not that appealing. But when the animation was put together, it was super smooth, energetic, and amazing. I always think that animators have some sort of otherworldly power to be able to think four-dimensionally.

HOW DO THE BREAKS YOU TAKE OFF FROM WORK REPLENISH YOUR MIND? I like to think of myself as a sponge when I take breaks. I go on trips, read books, watch movies, meet people, and just try to absorb as many different things as possible. Taking breaks is part of my job—I need the input to have the output.

Luke Jinks

After studying illustration in Bristol, Luke Jinks took an apprenticeship at the Infinite Ink Tattoo Studio Coventry to study traditional tattooing. This move is in keeping with the folklore, and Native American cultures, fifteenth-century royal paintings from Jodhpur, India, that influence his working style. He often chooses to ignore perspective in order to create a two-dimensional aesthetic with bold colors, and patterns. The artists whose work he admires includes Henry Gunderson, Margaret Kilgallen, Adam Hancher, Jonny Hannah, Jade Bridgwood, Jack Hudson, Owen Gatley, Bailey Hunter Robinson, Marcel Dzama, and Henry Darger.

Hollie Chastein

Collage artist Hollie Chastain scours antique shops in Chattanooga, Tennessee, for ideas and material for new work. Chipped paint, water stains, scribbles, mold spots, and natural textures and patterns inspire her nature-and-fairytale-influenced images.

She often waits for months just to find the perfect scrap of paper required for an idea, such as a coffee-stained book cover juxtaposed with a scrap of blue from a geography book at the bottom of a crate. She exhibits her work regularly at galleries across the world.

Page Tsou

1. _____ **Big Folk, 2011**
Imagem Production Music,
ALBUM * HAND DRAWN | DIGITAL

2. ___ **Alltogether Now, 2010**
Metro Taipei
BOOK * HAND DRAWN | COLLAGE | DIGITAL

3. _____ **Bus, 2010**
Metro Taipei
BOOK * HAND DRAWN | COLLAGE | DIGITAL

Page Tsou, originally
from Taiwan, is an
artist based in
London, UK. His work
is a mixture of hand
drawn collage and Digital, and has
been widely recognized including
being named Best of Show at the 2011
3x3 Professional Show and
the Bologna Children's Book Fair.

4_____ **Dancing Feathers, 2010**
Metro Taipei
BOOK * HAND DRAWN│COLLAGE│DIGITAL

5_____ **Sleepless, 2010**
Metro Taipei,
BOOK * HAND DRAWN│COLLAGE│DIGITAL

6_____ **Ray King, 2010**
Metro Taipei
BOOK * HAND DRAWN│COLLAGE│DIGITAL

7_____ **Egret, 2010**
Metro Taipei,
BOOK * HAND DRAWN│COLLAGE│DIGITAL

You Byun
—

1.   **The Moon, 2009**
Visual Arts Gallery
POSTER * MIXED MEDIA

2.   **Fly High Up, 2010**
Planadvisor Magazine
ART DIRECTOR: SOOJIN BUZELLI
EDITORIAL * DIGITAL

3.   **Goldielocks and Three Bears, 2010**
Plansponsor Magazine
EDITORIAL * DIGITAL

4.   **Make a Wish, 2010**
Plansponsor Magazine
SOOJIN BUZELLI
EDITORIAL * DIGITAL

5.   **Gifted, 2010**
Roger la Borde & Plansponsor Magazine
CREATIVE DIRECTORS : TIM SOLNICK (ROGER LA BORDE), SOOJIN BUZELLI (PLANSPONSOR MAGAZINE)
GREETING CARD & EDITORIAL * DIGITAL

You Byun was born in Queens, New York, and grew up between the United States, Japan, and Korea before moving back to New York to work as an illustrator. She likes to draw girls, birds, and monsters, and place these characters in lush, nostalgic environments. From her studio in Brooklyn, she works on editorial assignments, gallery pieces, books, and stationery. Her first children's book, DREAM FRIENDS, will be published by Penguin Books. Matisse, Takashi Murakam, Kiki Smith, and Yuko Shimizu are just some of the many artists whose work she admires.

Katie Scott

1. _____ **Vision, 2011**
   Personal
   POSTER • HAND DRAWN |
   WATERCOLOR | DIGITAL

2. _____ **Organs, 2011**
   Personal
   POSTER • HAND DRAWN |
   WATERCOLOR | DIGITAL

3. _____ **Rocks, 2011**
   Personal
   POSTER • HAND DRAWN |
   WATERCOLOR | DIGITAL

4. _____ **Mind, 2011**
   Personal
   POSTER • HAND DRAWN |
   WATERCOLOR | DIGITAL

U.K. illustrator Katie Scott is interested in: Jean Rouch, Sergei Parajanov, wizard fiction, John Wyndham, palms, pineapples, sonic booms, L.A.R.P., body builders, and beach babes. And Edo-period Japanese medical illustration. Her style recalls vintage biological illustrations used in field guides and educational manuals, though the creatures it depicts do not appear to be of this world. Her most recent project is a catalog of flora and fauna from Jules Verne's novel JOURNEY TO THE CENTER OF THE EARTH.

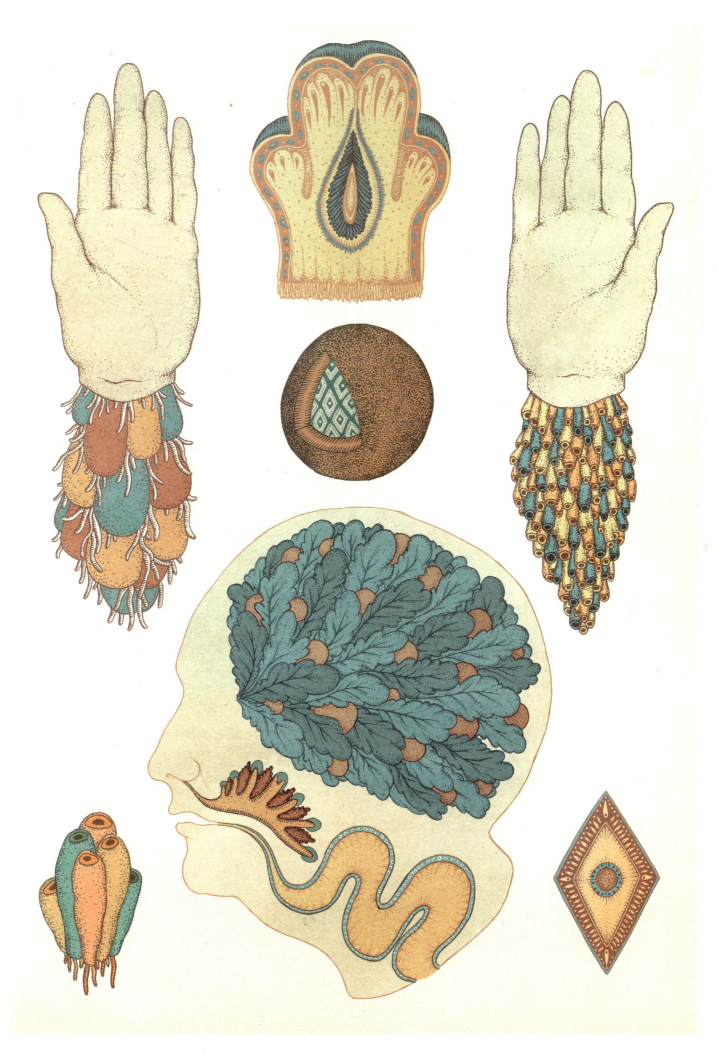

Álvaro
Laura

1.|2.|3. **Guías dos Rios**
e Barragens-Lima, 2011
Visão Viagens Magazine
ART DIRECTION: JONAS REKER
COVER * HAND DRAWN | DIGITAL

4. **We're the mods,**
we're the mods!, 2010
Personal
POSTER * HAND DRAWN | DIGITAL

5.|6.|7. **Retiro Park Muppet**
Theater, 2010
Madrid City Council
Arts Department
ART DIRECTION: ROBERTO LEICEAGA
VISUAL IDENTITY *
HAND DRAWN | DIGITAL

The Berlin-based
illustrator Álvaro Laura
was born in Burgos,
Spain, in 1977. After
studying fine arts
and graphic design (with a focus in
advertising) in Salamanca, he worked
as a designer and illustrator in Spain,
Portugal, and Germany, creating work
both by hand and with the computer
that has appeared in books and
magazines. After publishing his first
comic book in 2007, he decided to work
full time as an illustrator in Berlin,
where he could also be close to his
beloved. In addition to commercial
jobs, he illustrates children's books,
and makes time to collaborate on
projects with other artists. He can also
be found learning German, playing
the guitar, and nursing the wounds he
inflicts on himself while
skateboarding.

Lindsey Carr

The artist—and sometimes toy maker—Lindsey Carr lives and works on the southwest coast of Scotland. Her work is greatly influenced by European and Chinese natural history paintings of the eighteenth and nineteenth centuries. Each of her pieces is gradually built up with layers of watercolor and ink on paper. Some pieces are further embellished with decorative materials, such as gold leaf.

1. **Garden, 2010**
Personal
WATERCOLOUR|ACRYLIC

2. **Ortus, 2011**
Personal
WATERCOLOUR|ACRYLIC

3. **Dolens Fecund, 2011**
Personal
WATERCOLOUR|ACRYLIC

4. **La Bizarre Singerie, 2010**
Personal
WATERCOLOUR|ACRYLIC

5. **Great Hornbill, 2010**
Personal
WATERCOLOUR|ACRYLIC

Lisel Ashlock

New York City-based illustrator and designer Lisel Ashlock is always on the hunt for the perfect piece of birch wood to paint on. Bruce Springsteen, old family photos, Diamond Lake in Spokane, her tiny garden in Brooklyn, summer bike rides, Andrew Wyeth, Frida Kahlo, Waldon Ford, Henry Darger, Balthus, Edward Gorey, Rackam, Dulac, Kay Neilsen have all found their way into her work. Penguin Books, The Audobon Society, Sony, PLAYBOY, and SPIN MAGAZINE are just some of her clients. She has been featured in COMMUNICATION ARTS, AMERICAN ILLUSTRATION, and 3x3.

Earth Day 2010

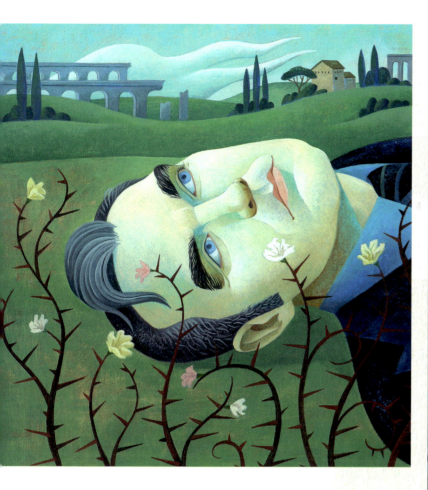

Jody Hewgill

1. **Earth Day 2010, 2009**
The United States
Department of State
ART DIRECTOR: DIANE WOOLVERTON
POSTER FOR DISTRIBUTION IN US
CONSULATES AND EMBASSIES AROUND
THE WORLD. * ACRYLIC

2. **The Roman Spring**
of Mr. Morrissey, 2006
Spin Magazine
ART DIRECTOR: DEVIN PEDZWATER
EDITORIAL * ACRYLIC

3. **Tender Morsels**
by Margo Lanagan, 2008
Knopf
ART DIRECTOR: ISABEL WARREN LYNCH
BOOK COVER * ACRYLIC

4. **Notorious, 2008**
Uppercase
CREDITS: JANINE VANGOOL,
ORIGINALLY COMMISSIONED
BY MARK MURPHY
EDITORIAL/EXHIBITION * ACRYLIC

A native of Montréal, Québec, Jody currently teaches illustration in the graduate program at the Ontario College of Art and Design in Toronto. She has worked on a wide variety of assignments and commissions including book covers, celebrity portraits, theater posters, and retail interior murals for clients in North America, Europe, and Asia. Her paintings have been commissioned by the Atlanta Olympic Committee, ENTERTAINMENT WEEKLY, OPRAH MAGAZINE, ROLLING STONE, TIME, and the US Department of State. AMERICAN ILLUSTRATION, COMMUNICATION ARTS, PRINT MAGAZINE, The Society of Publication Designers, the Society of Illustrators in New York and Los Angeles have honored her work and a series of her posters are included in the Permanent Poster Collection of the Library of Congress in Washington, D.C. Private and public collections throughout North America and Europe include her work.

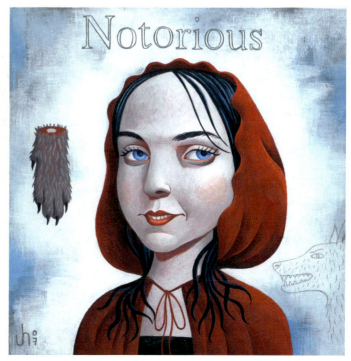

1. _____ **Every Tongue Confess**
by Marcus Gardley, 2010
Arena Stage
ART DIRECTOR : NICKY LINDEMAN,
CREATIVE DIRECTOR: GAIL ANDERSON,
AGENCY: SPOTCO
POSTER AND BROCHURE * ACRYLIC

2. _____ **Drivin' n Cryin', 2010**
Personal
EXHIBITION PIECE * ACRYLIC|GRAPHITE

3. _____ **Ambivalent, 2009**
Personal
EXHIBITION PIECE * ACRYLIC

4. _____ **Portrait of a Lady with**
Fox, 2006
Personal
EXHIBITION PIECE * ACRYLIC

Chris Buzelli

1. **Aging Tyger, 2010**
   ai5000 Magazine
   ART DIRECTOR: SOOJIN BUZELLI
   EDITORIAL * OIL ON PANEL

2. **Abracadabra, 2010**
   Personal
   EXHIBITION PIECE * OIL ON PANEL

3. **Murky Waters, 2009**
   Plansponsor Magazine
   ART DIRECTOR: SOOJIN BUZELLI
   EDITORIAL * OIL ON PAPER

4. **Darkest Day, 2009**
   Illumination Magazine
   ART DIRECTOR: BLAKE DINSDALE
   EDITORIAL * OIL ON PAPER

5. **Flight, 2009**
   Plansponsor Magazine
   ART DIRECTOR: SOOJIN BUZELLI
   EDITORIAL * GRAPHITE | OIL ON PAPER

Chris Buzelli was born and raised outside of Chicago, USA, on the waters of Lake Michigan. Starting at a young age, Buzelli painted side by side with his grandfather, Armondo Buzelli, who became a great influence on his work. His oil paintings have appeared in many national and international publications including ROLLING STONE, PLAYBOY, the VILLAGE VOICE, NEW YORK TIMES, LA TIMES, and BOSTON GLOBE. Buzelli has also collaborated on numerous projects for design firms, advertising agencies, and Broadway musical posters. He has exhibited his work at galleries throughout North America.

Marco Wagner

Marco Wagner is from the small Bavarian town of Würzburg, Germany. Since 2006, he has worked as an artist and illustrator in Veitshöchheim using a mix of techniques such as acrylic, pencil, cut paper, crayons, and the computer. His images have a dark undertone to them, mixing realistic elements with abstract situations. Contemporary artists whose work he admires include David Hughes, Lars Henkel, Nicoletta Ceccoli, Olaf Hajek, and Camilla Engman.
A finalist for the European Design Awards in 2008, Wagner's work is also the recipient of numerous honors and has been published internationally.

1. **Heimat gerne, 2011**
Lucid Dreams Exhibition
CURATOR: MARK MURPHY
EXHIBITION PIECE * MIXED MEDIA

2. **Maria, 2011**
Galerie Neongolden
CURATOR: PETRA BERMES
EXHIBITION PIECE * MIXED MEDIA

3. **Herec, 2010**
Personal
EXHIBITION PIECE * MIXED MEDIA

4. **Brigitte, 2010**
Schaf mit fünf Pfoten Exhibition
CURATOR: ANNETTE GLOSER
EXHIBITION PIECE * MIXED MEDIA

5. **Bin im Park, 2010**
Survey Select Exhibition
CURATOR: MARK MURPHY
EXHIBITION PIECE * MIXED MEDIA

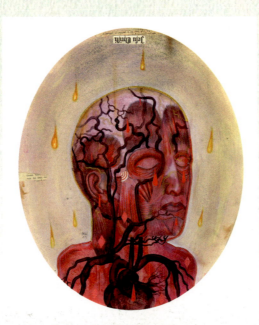

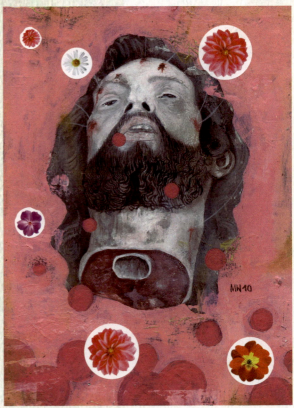

1   **Bin im Wald, 2010**
Survey Select Exhibition
CURATOR: MARK MURPHY
EXHIBITION PIECE * ACRYLIC

2   **Der Hund, 2010**
Schaf mit fünf Pfoten
Exhibition
CURATOR: ANNETTE GLOSER
EXHIBITION PIECE * MIXED MEDIA

3   **Pomery, 2010**
Personal
PAINTING * MIXED MEDIA

4   **Traditionell, 2011**
Galerie Neongolden
CURATOR: PETRA BERMES
EXHIBITION PIECE * MIXED MEDIA

5   **Es war 1921, 2010**
Personal
PAINTING * ACRYLIC

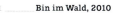

John Dyer Baizley

As the singer and guitarist for the rock band Baroness, John Baizley has toured the world and released several critically acclaimed albums. As an artist, John has created the cover art for all of Baroness's releases, as well as classic albums such as FLIGHT OF THE CONCHORDS. Baizley's lush artwork shows the influence of two major artists: Pushead's morbid subject matter and fine penwork, and Alphonse Mucha's graceful composition of his subjects in art deco scenes. He is currently based in Philadelphia.

WHAT KIND OF PLACE DID YOU GROW UP IN? I grew up in a small town called Lexington, Virginia, up in the mountains—a very rural, very pastoral kind of place. But there wasn't anything much that interested me there, and there was little to do anyway. You either played sports or worked on your parent's farm or you just got into trouble—I tried all of them, and nothing gave me the mental or physical sustenance that I needed. When you turn into a teenager and you're at that angsty, angry stage that happens in adolescence, kids I knew ended up fucking themselves up, either in jail or with substance abuse problems. My art and my creative drive was what kept me relatively grounded in a place where dangerous situations were born out of sheer boredom. So I just made art and started playing music—it wasn't conscious by any means, it wasn't like I thought to myself, I'll make art and play music and that'll keep me out of trouble. I just wanted to give myself something to do.

WHAT KIND OF EFFECT DID GROWING UP IN SUCH A RURAL ENVIRONMENT HAVE ON YOUR WORK? The art and music is not really a product of my environment, but more of a reflection of the environment that I was in.

WHAT WAS THE FIRST THING YOU STARTED DRAWING? My mother, from an early age, recognized that I had that spark or whatever, a "creative type" kid. She and my father both had something between a passing or amateur interest in art, meaning they both studied it in college and they knew their way around a piece of paper and a sketchbook. My mother saw it as an opportunity to push me or allow me to do something that I was interested in. From an age where I had no memory, she was encouraging anything artistic that I did, buying supplies and whatnot—she even bought me a little guitar when I was six. So I never felt like this type of life was something I couldn't do.

YOUR LINES ARE VERY SOLID BUT YET YOU USE WATERCOLOR, AN INHERENTLY UNSTABLE MEDIUM. IS THAT YOUR WAY OF GIVING UP CONTROL IN A WAY? Yeah, well, that gets right to the problem: my art is built out of a nervousness and anxiety, and yet I work in this very controlled, precision-based medium. It's ink! Working the way that I do, it's tough to add any type of spontaneity to a line—once it's there, it's there. So, through watercolor, I'm always trying to imbue my image with a sense of life and energy or spontaneity, but it's tough to do that. That's why I find that creating these black-and-white images in order to exemplify the utmost to which I can control myself, to which I can focus on one thing more than a few seconds, and once I've got that, I add the watercolor: here's the magic, here's the stuff I can't control. From a technical standpoint, though, I have to admit I don't know what I'm doing. It's a medium full of beautiful, unintentional mistakes. I'm not filling in black lines with broad sheets of color—that just feels too comic-booky. So I'm trying to be as painterly as possible but still get the point across. If I try to describe what I do, people say that's not making "art," it's making "illustration," and it's not my interest to be an "illustrator"—everything I do is to put this control into a thing, and then blow it out with some spontaneity.

WHAT'S NEXT FOR THE BAND? We're putting out a record out in the next few months and the first part of the process is making the music, and then I get to make art for the music. I'm trying to do something a little bit grander than what I've done in the past. And I've just finished an album cover for Gillian Welch.

HOW DID THAT COME ABOUT? Well, I'm a true fan of her music, and what she does in that realm is what appeals to me. It's very much not pop, it's very non-conformist, and the fact that she has become a popular artist while flying in the face of contemporary popular music is interesting to me. And her content is dark—death and abuse, the stuff we're supposed to write songs about. Not this frilly surface stuff.

DID YOU HAVE SOME ENCOURAGEMENT TO GO TO RISD? I had teachers who encouraged me, but there was no real recognition that it could be a viable career. Early on, I realized that I had to do something different from what the other people in school were doing. I had this interest in creation, in making things, making sounds, making art—of course, I wasn't a very good musician at the time, I just loved doing it. So, what was left was art school. I applied to a million of them and I visited Baltimore and Chicago and Los Angeles, and as a 16 year old, I was like, these places look awesome and this is where I want to be. At the time, these schools were the most expensive schools in America. I didn't understand that art school was more for privileged kids.

DID YOU SHOW UP TO ART SCHOOL WITH YOUR STYLE FULLY FORMED? Oh no, where I grew up, there weren't museums to go to, so I got into art through music, and over time I figured out a blend of what feels like to me is so-called fine art and art from music, and album covers. I guess you'd call it commercial illustration but I consider it my art.

HAVE YOU BEGUN TO DO ANY WORK USING DIGITAL TOOLS OR IS IT ALL STILL HAND-DRAWN? I spent my entire schooling using traditional media, and that's where I'm comfortable and where I feel familiar, and that's why my work comes along pretty slowly. When I have to deliver something and trust it to someone else, I scan it in and send it over. But it feels really awkward to me when I take something that I've finished in real time in the analog world, and then turn it into something digital and alter it, and make it better—that doesn't seem like how it should work for me. It feels inorganic.

1. **Deliver Us, 2007**
The Darkest Hour
RECORD COVER • WATERCOLOR | INK

2. **Static Tensions, 2009**
Kylesa
RECORD COVER • WATERCOLOR | INK

3. **Femme, 2010**
Baroness
PAINTING • WATERCOLOR | INK

Allison Torneros

1. _____ **Lotus Blossom, 2008**
Personal
ACRYLIC

2. _____ **Breakeven, 2009**
Private Commission
POSTER * ACRYLIC

3. _____ **Reflecting On Peculiar Events, 2009**
Personal
ACRYLIC | INK

4. _____ **The City, 2006**
Personal
POSTER * ACRYLIC |
MARKER | COLORED PENCIL

The Los Angeles-based illustrator and designer Allison Torneros formed her studio, CircleDot, in 2008. Her clients include Disney, Procter&Gamble, and DreamWorks, and The North Face, with whom she worked recently on a series of graphic bags and apparel. Competitive by nature, she has appeared on MTV's reality show and digital arts competition, Engine Room, and competed in the Cut & Paste SF 2009 Digital Design Tournament, where she won first place and the people's choice award. Torneros is a self-proclaimed geek, dance machine, and expert in all things Michael Jackson, working happily in her studio in Los Angeles, USA.

Estela A. Cuadro

1.|2.|3.|4._____ **Mujeres**
Coquetas 1–4, 2011
Personal
MIXED MEDIA

Argentinean-born Estela A. Cuadro uses bold colors and shapes in her work that is a process of deliberate planning and intuitive decision-making. The history and current economical problems of Argentina are an inspiration to her work because it requires people to think creatively about finding solutions and creating new ideas. She admires the work of artists such as Pablo Picasso, Egon Schiele, Amy Cutler, Gustav Klimt, and Xul Solar.

Enric Borràs

Margarita Xirgú

Boom Artwork

Boom Artwork is also Eric van den Boom, a freelance graphic designer who specializes in illustration and custom lettering. He works from studio in Utrecht in the Netherlands. His illustration work is often described as strong and detailed, vintage with a modern look, authentic and elegant with an edge. His inspiration is found in daily life, contemporary art, music, film, friends, and the great history of art. Combining traditional techniques with contemporary technology, water colors with markers, biros, spirographs, compasses, etc., van den Boom produces a wide range of illustrative design work for advertising, cultural markets, fashion, editorial, and the music industry, including MTV Networks, and Ray Ban.

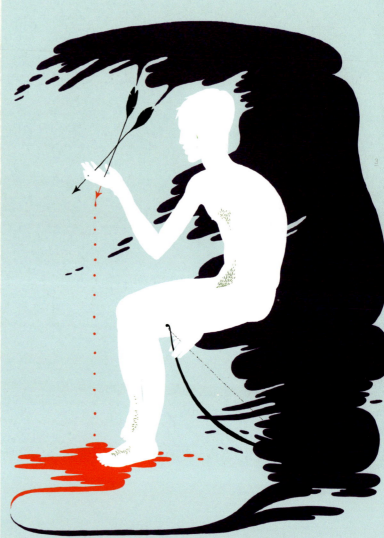

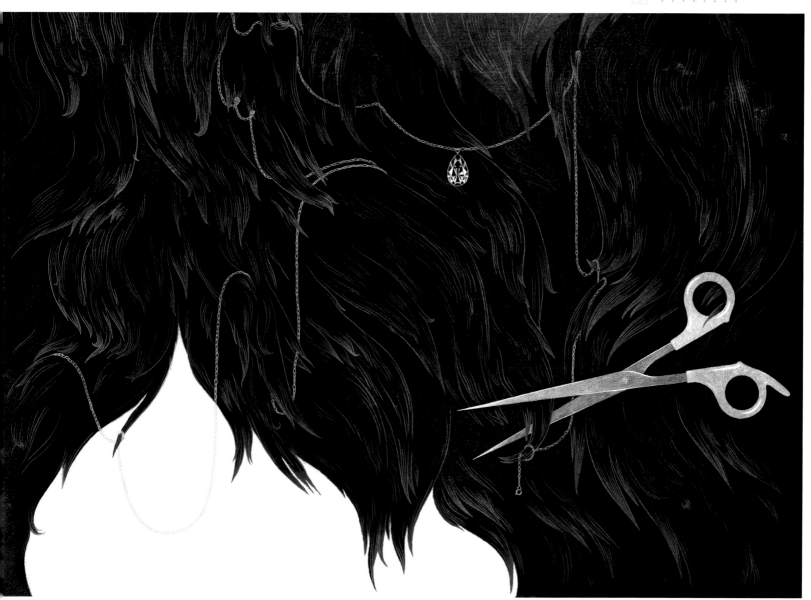

Micah Lidberg

Micah Lidberg's midwestern upbringing in Kansas City, Missouri, meant that he was raised amongst fields, and forests, and polite people. In addition to being influenced by this landscape, he names Mike Perry and Mario Hugo as just two of many artists whose work he admires. He uses a mechanical pencil, paper, and the computer to create illustrations that have been commissioned by clients such as Nike, the NEW YORK TIMES MAGAZINE, and NYLON magazine. After self-publishing a number of zines, his book Rise & Fall: A CONCERTINA OF LIFE was published by Nobrow in 2010. His interests include—but are not limited to—drawing, friends, people, America, places outside of America, strangeness, and occasionally tea.

Irana Douer

The Argentinean artist Irana Douer creates colorful work that consists of many techniques and styles. She is editor of the online art magazine RUBY, which brings her into contact with hundreds of other artists. Her book, RUBY: OTHERWORLDLINESS, was published in 2011.

1. **Untitled (Escondida), 2011**
Personal
MALEVO ESTAMPA (LUCIANO MURÚA TOLCACHIER + ANA WINGEYER)
HAND COLORED ETCHING

2. **Untitled (Cabello con Flores), 2011**
Personal
MALEVO ESTAMPA (LUCIANO MURÚA TOLCACHIER + ANA WINGEYER)
HAND COLORED ETCHING

3. **Cat Dagger, 2011**
Blood is the New Black
T-SHIRT * HAND DRAWN

4. **Untitled, 2010**
Personal
ACRYLIC PAINT AND PENCIL ON PAPER

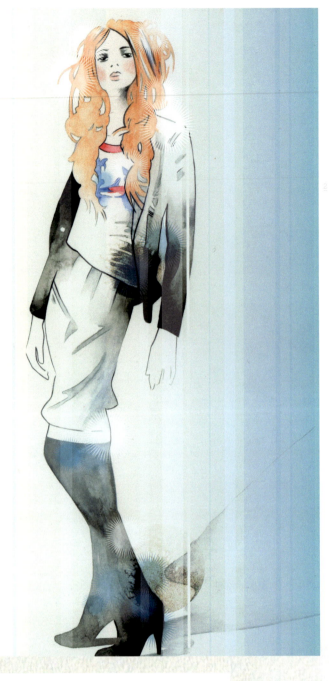

Nadia Flower

Fragile and delicate but also graphic and strong—these elements define Nadia Flower's illustration work. From her studio in New Zealand, she works for clients across the world, applying hand-drawn, and computer-based imagery to a range of visual mediums including fashion, editorial, advertising, books, and textiles. Her clients include Lily Allen, Fornarina, NYLON magazine, GHD, Coca-Cola, GLAMOUR UK, Saatchi & Saatchi, MARIE CLAIRE, YEN magazine, Graniph, Zoe and Morgan, and Bourjois.

1. **Intangled, 2007**
Fornarina
CLOTHING * HAND DRAWN | WATERCOLOR | DIGITAL

2. **High Fashion 1, 2009**
Personal
HAND DRAWN | WATERCOLOR | DIGITAL

3. **High Fashion 2, 2008**
Personal
HAND DRAWN | WATERCOLOR | DIGITAL

4. **Young At Heart, 2010**
Personal
HAND DRAWN | WATERCOLOR | DIGITAL

5. **The Beast and Me, 2009**
Camaieu
PRINTED CARDS * HAND DRAWN | WATERCOLOR | DIGITAL

Andre Sanchez

Using a mixture of photography, typography, and textures, Paris-based Andre Sanchez creates brightly colored illustrations for use in print, editorial, and music projects for clients such as Condé Nast, Le Monde, Dr. Martens, Warner Music, and Sony Music. He is also cofounder and editor of Web Culture, an online magazine of alternative culture.

1. **Esse Quam Videri, 2011**
Personal
PRINT ON ALIMINIUM * DIGITAL|
PICTURES|TYPO|TEXTURES|ENGRAVINGS

2. **Post Tenebras Lux, 2011**
Personal
PRINT ON ALIMINIUM * DIGITAL|
PICTURES|TYPO|TEXTURES|ENGRAVINGS

3. **Truth Alone Triumphs, 2011**
Personal
PRINT ON ALIMINIUM * DIGITAL|
PICTURES|TYPO|TEXTURES|ENGRAVINGS

4. **Sub Umbra Floreo, 2011**
Personal
PRINT ON ALIMINIUM * DIGITAL|
PICTURES|TYPO|TEXTURES|ENGRAVINGS

5. **Semper Pro Grediens, 2011**
Personal
PRINT ON ALIMINIUM * DIGITAL|
PICTURES|TYPO|TEXTURES|ENGRAVINGS

Tugboat Printshop

Paul Roden and Valerie Lueth are the husband and wife team behind Tugboat Printshop. Since 2006, they have been working together to create contemporary artwork using traditional printmaking techniques. Their work combines Lueth's intricate drawings, etchings, and block prints with Roden's large-scale narrative pieces—and sometimes collaborations with other artists. Each print is made with top-shelf, oil-based inks printed on archival paper. Tugboat Printshop is based in Pittsburgh, USA.

Apfel Zet

Apfel Zet was founded in 1997. At the core of their client base are cultural institutions, publishing houses, and design labels including DIE ZEIT and American Express. An independent comic book and a website about two fictional cities are personal projects that keep their practice fresh and highlight the theme of architecture that can be seen throughout their work. Ott & Stein, Edward Hopper, Chris Ware, Winsor McCay, Hergé, and Ludwig Hohlwein are a few of their influences.
In addition to creating graphics and illustration, Apfel Zet has written theoretical articles on design and architecture for a number of publications.

5). Dachs

4). *Waschbär*

6). *Murmeltier*

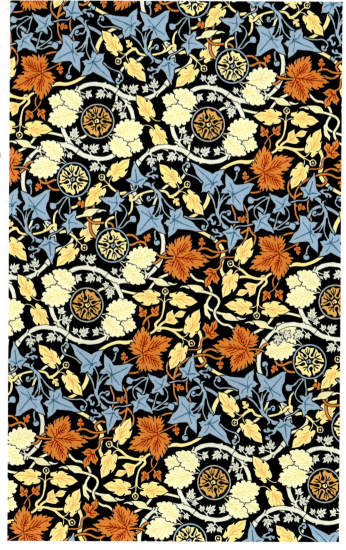

1 **Newarc, 2010**
Direktorenhaus Berlin
WALLPAPER • DIGITAL

2 **Brighton, 2010**
Direktorenhaus Berlin
WALLPAPER • DIGITAL

3 **Blackpool, 2009**
Direktorenhaus Berlin
WALLPAPER • DIGITAL

4 **Marburg, 2010**
Bayer | Uhrig Architects,
WALLPAPER • DIGITAL

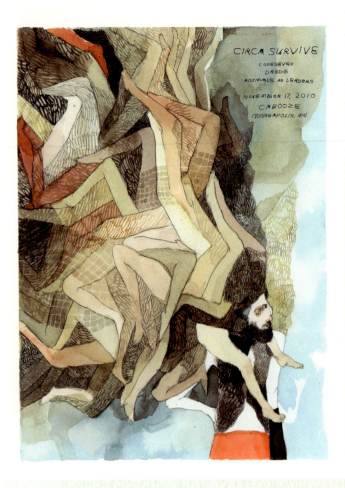

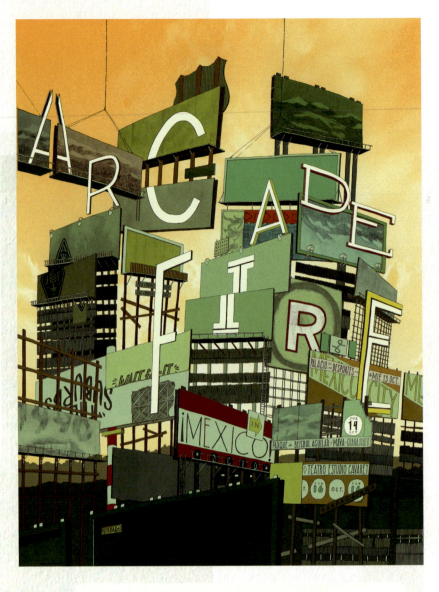

LandLand

—

Landland is a small graphic design and illustration studio in Minneapolis, USA, run by Dan Black and Jessica Seamans. They create record sleeves, posters, and art prints with computers, scanners, photocopiers, drawings, screen printing, or whatever it takes to get the job done. Upcoming projects include publishing short-run books, and a handful of limited-edition records.

1. **Circa Survive in Minneapolis, Minn., 2010**
Circa Survive
GIG POSTER * WATERCOLOR |
SCREENPRINT * ILLUSTRATOR:
JESSICA SEAMANS

2. **Arcade Fire's Mexico Tour, 2010**
Arcade Fire
TOUR POSTER * HAND DRAWN |
SCREENPRINT * ILLUSTRATOR:
DAN BLACK * PRINT: BEN LAFOND /
BURLESQUE OF NORTH AMERICA

3. **The Appleseed Cast in Dekalb, Ill., 2010**
The Appleseed Cast
GIG POSTER *
HAND DRAWN | SCREENPRINT
ILLUSTRATOR: DAN BLACK

4. **The Swell Season in St. Louis, Miss., 2009**
The Swell Season
GIG POSTER * WATERCOLOR |
SCREENPRINT * ILLUSTRATORS:
DAN BLACK & JESSICA SEAMANS

5. **Iron & Wine U.S. Tour, 2011**
Iron & Wine
TOUR POSTER * HAND DRAWN |
WATERCOLOR | SCREENPRINT *
ILLUSTRATOR: JESSICA SEAMANS

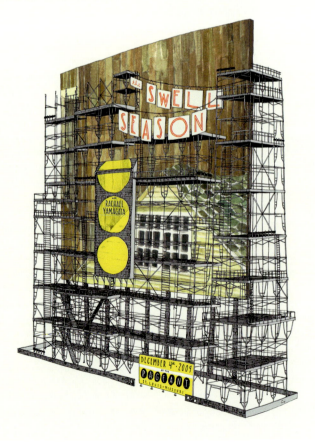

Phasianus versicolor

Chris Turnham

1. ___ **Green Pheasant, 2010**
Personal
HAND DRAWN | DIGITAL

2. ___ **The Hazards of Love, 2009**
The Decemberists
TOUR POSTER * DIGITAL | SCREENPRINT

3. ___ **Discovery, 2008**
Personal
HAND DRAWN | DIGITAL

4. ___ **Winter Flowers, 2010**
Personal
HAND DRAWN | DIGITAL

Mid-century illustrators, the Disney greats like Mary Blair, Eyvind Earle, and Walt Peregoy, Martin and Alice Provensen, Andrew Wyeth, and Tadahiro Uesugi are on the list of influences of Chris Turnham's work. Turnham has worked as an illustrator for clients such as Monocle and Scholastic. His atmospheric environments have also been used in video games and by animation studios, most notably for the film Coraline. He lives and works in Los Angeles, USA.

Tomer Hanuka

Tomer Hanuka, an illustrator and cartoonist based in New York City, was raised in Ramat-Ilan, an enclave of high-rises outside of Tel-Aviv, Israel. He has worked on a range of projects for magazines, book publishers, ad agencies, and film studios; and his clients include THE NEW YORKER, DC Comics, MTV, Nike, and Microsoft. The Society of Illustrators and the Society of Publication Designers have honored his work, and in 2008, he won the British Design Museum Award. WALTZ WITH BASHIR, an animated documentary for which Hanuka contributed art, was nominated for an Oscar and won the Golden Globe in 2009. He currently teaches at the School of Visual Arts in New York, and is working on a graphic novel, THE DIVINE, with his twin brother Asaf and the writer Boaz Lavie. OVERKILL, a monograph of his work from the last ten years, will be out this fall; HARD APPLE, an animated show based on a series of crime novels by Jerome Charyn, is in development.

WHAT WAS IT ABOUT GROWING UP IN ISRAEL THAT INFLUENCED YOUR INTEREST IN ILLUSTRATION? The prescribed mythology of the local culture at the time mostly revolved around war heroes, generals, pieces of land, and religious landmarks. As a boy, I had zero interest in those. I was enchanted by anything that came from outside of Israel, and comics suggested a different mythology, less painful, and rooted in fantasy rather than reality. It worked my imagination in a completely different way.

HOW DID YOU LEARN TO DRAW? My twin brother, Asaf, and I were assembling a fantastic universe together, drawing together, reading together, a two-man operation trying to lead an alternate childhood. The longing to live inside the panels created a need to construct our own panels. Only years later came art school, figure drawing, the rejection of anything genre, and the eventual re-embracing.

ABOUT HOW OLD WERE YOU THEN? We were probably around six or seven. Superman and Batman were the gateway drug—perfectly embodying what boys lack at a certain age: a sense of being powerful and a clear origin story.

SO THEY WERE EXPLICITLY NOT POLITICAL? No, they were superhero fantasies for young boys—that was the subversive element, diving into a world that was so completely irrelevant to the day-to-day reality of living in Israel.

YOU'VE SAID THAT YOU DIDN'T REALLY DEVELOP YOUR PERSONAL VOICE UNTIL ABOUT SIX MONTHS AFTER SCHOOL. My last year of college, I put together a portfolio that I thought clients would appreciate, which is the wrong way to go about anything—trying to predict expectations. I had kept drawing comics in a way that never felt like a "style," just as a utilitarian way of telling a story with minimal embellishment. After graduation, I met with Gerald Rapp, one of the biggest agents at the time, for a portfolio review. Among the painterly stuff I had included, I had one comics cover done with a black line brush and flat colors, nothing I would ever show to magazines. He suggested I create an entire portfolio using my "comics" approach. And he was right. I never painted again.

WHAT WAS SO INFLUENTIAL ABOUT PEOPLE LIKE LORENZO MATTOTTI OR TADANORI YOKOO? Mattotti is a dramatic storyteller with an orchestra of emotions and subtleties. And he is a bold image-maker. There is an energy that follows the action, and when Mattotti completely harnesses that energy—coupled with his insights and humanity—the effect is rich and satisfying. Yokoo's colors open up a new space in my head. The combinations, arrangements, and effects all seem to clash and confront the viewer's assumptions about harmony and structure.
His posters somehow manage to be both aesthetically offensive and reaffirming. Each image is a small initiation experience.

HOW ARE YOUR ANIMATED PIECES SIMILAR OR DIFFERENT FROM YOUR PRINT WORK? It's about the group dynamic. I'm a link in a chain, doing my best, but then you have to let it go. Collaboration is a terrific thing, and art is a conversation.
There is something blessedly unpredictable about giving up full control.

WHAT IS YOUR FAVORITE THING TO DRAW? The back of the head, because I struggle to get them to look right.

WHY IS THAT? It's a deceptively three-dimensional shape. It seems flat for some reason, maybe as an extension of the back, as opposed to the face were there is so much emphasis. But it actually has its own specific shape, and can be extremely expressive.

DO YOU CREATE YOUR IMAGES ENTIRELY BY HAND OR IS IT A COMBINATION OF DIGITAL AND HAND-DRAWN ELEMENTS? The drawing is handmade, and the colors are digital. I still feel that color is a great silent weapon. It is the unknown part of the execution. If the general concept of a piece is a destination, and the line drawing is a blueprint, then the color is a joker—I can never predict what colors will work or where. I never provide color sketches for instance. It's a death sentence for the process.

HOW SO? The drawing, in my case, is like a Golem. It needs the spark of a soul, something that will animate it from a static object into a living thing. Color is that spark.

Chokeshin

Zoe Lacchei

Zoe Lacchei's childhood home, a small, isolated town near Rome, nurtured in her a love of abstraction and escapism, which now forms the basis of her work. Her love of human anatomy and Japanese culture also comes through in her work, which has been published and exhibited. She has created artwork for Marilyn Manson's albums THE GOLDEN AGE OF THE GROTESQUE and EAT ME, DRINK ME. Since 2007 she has been the owner of a studio-gallery in Rome.

Louise
Robinson

Amongst the many things
and people that influence
Louise Robinson's work
are Jung, Paula Rego, gothic
fiction, surrealism, folklore,
playing cards, Monty Python, David
Lynch, and Miss Marple. She creates
her imagery digitally with a Wacom
tablet, Digital, and a combination of
watercolor, acrylic, pencil, and hand-
drawn text. Her paintings involve color
mixing and blending with added
textures that create depth, while the
illustrative works take the form
of line drawings and are primarily
concerned with pattern, design,
and fine detail.

4

5

6

7

Jörn Kaspuhl

Jörn Kaspuhl was born in Stade, a town near Hamburg, Germany. Before his graduation from the University of Applied Sciences Hamburg in October 2008, he had already gained experience working as a freelance illustrator for several local and international magazines, publishers, musicians, and fashion labels. His client list is continuously growing, including such names as the NEW YORKER, MONOCLE, GQ, the INDEPENDENT, WIRED, DIE ZEIT, and DER SPIEGEL. He lives and works near the harbor in Hamburg.

Tyler Stout

Tyler Stout was born and raised in Washington State, just across the river from Portland, Oregon. His work, which mixes realistic and cartoonish styles, was most recently used by Marvel Comics for the new CAPTAIN AMERICA. Stout begins his work by hand, always converting it into a digital format before sending it on to the client. Some inspirations to his work are considered to be Mobius, Bernie Wrightson, Frank Miller, Dave Gibbons, Frank Miller, Mike Mignola, Tony Moore, and the comic book series THE LAST MAN. He's also been known to buy science fiction paperbacks just for the cover artwork—and end up reading them, too.

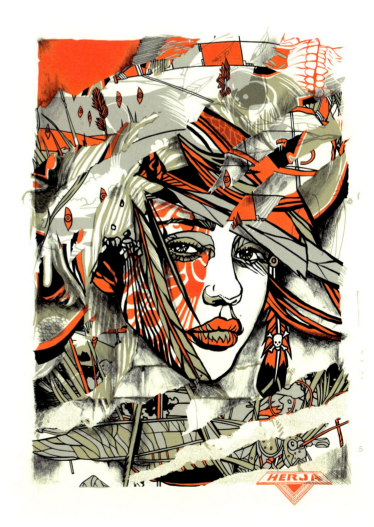

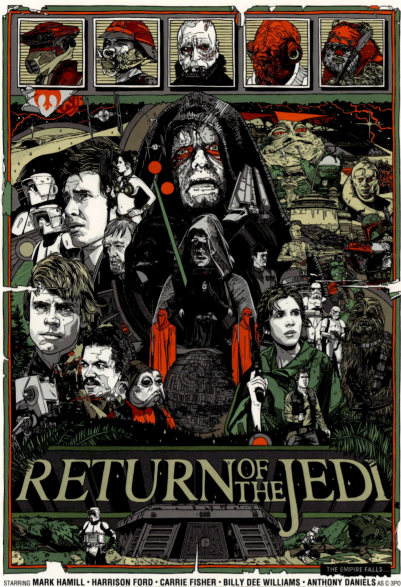

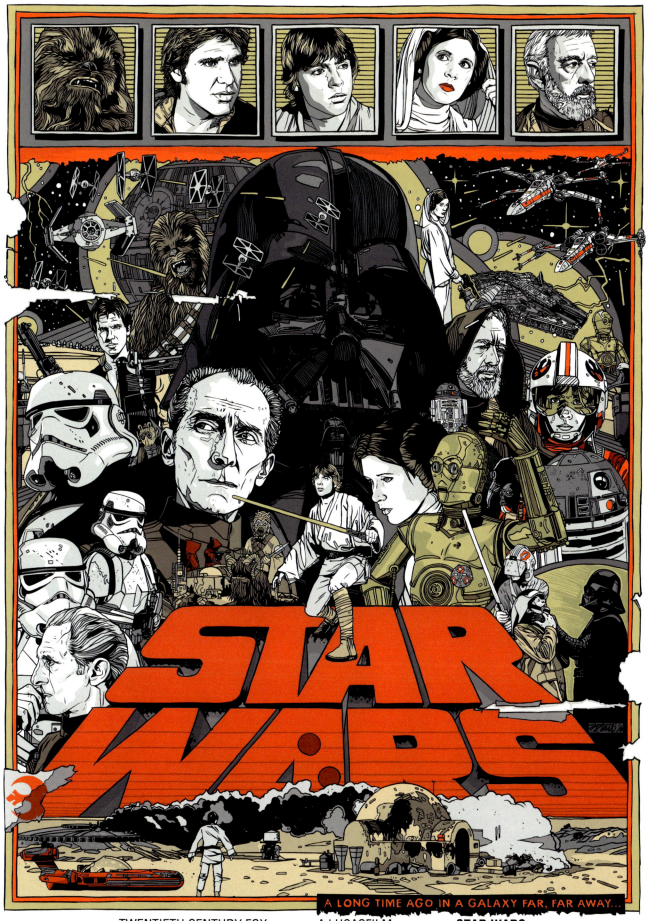

A LONG TIME AGO IN A GALAXY FAR, FAR AWAY...

TWENTIETH CENTURY FOX PRESENTS A LUCASFILM PRODUCTION STAR WARS
STARRING **MARK HAMILL · HARRISON FORD · CARRIE FISHER · PETER CUSHING** AND **ALEC GUINNESS**
WRITTEN AND DIRECTED BY GEORGE LUCAS PRODUCED BY GARY KURTZ MUSIC BY JOHN WILLIAMS
PANAVISION · TECHNICOLOR · PRINTS BY DE LUXE

Making Films Sound Better
DOLBY SYSTEM
Noise Reduction · High Fidelity

Simón Prades

1.-3.____ **Chaos und Ordnung:**
I, II, III, 2010
Personal
EXHIBITION PIECE * INK

4.|5.____ **Mexico I + II, 2010**
Personal
EXHIBITION PIECE *
INK|WATERCOLOR|DIGITAL

From his home in Trier, Germany, illustrator and graphic designer Simón Prades uses ink, watercolor, and Digital to create illustrations and book designs. His recent work has been inspired by the old technique of etching because it combines the sensibility of drawing with precise handcraft. Whenever possible, he works in analog techniques before using the computer to finish the work.

Sandra Diekmann

1. **Mr. Ragdoll Cat, 2010**
Private Commission
PRINT * PEN | PENCIL | DIGITAL

2. **Grizzly, 2010**
Personal
PRINT * PEN | PENCIL | DIGITAL

3. **Wolf Mask, 2010**
Gabby Young
& Other Animals
POSTER * PEN | PENCIL | DIGITAL

4. **The White Bison, 2011**
Personal
PRINT * PEN | PENCIL | DIGITAL

Growing up, Sandra Dieckmann was surrounded by nature in her tiny village of Oldenburg, Germany. The influence of nature has stayed with her and her work, even after her 2002 move to London, where she now lives and works; her images revolve around nature, wildlife, dreams, and observations. It was during her studies of fashion design that she discovered illustration and developed a style that is detailed, colorful, patterned, and partly graphic using tools that include pen, pencil, ink, collage, and digital editing. She counts anything by David Attenborough as an influence as well as nature books, Google image searches for animals, bus dreaming, and music.

Jeannie Phan

1. **Yoko's Toys, 2010**
Personal
EDITORIAL * PENCIL|DIGITAL

2. **Lungs, 2011**
Personal
POSTER * PAINT|PENCIL|DIGITAL

3. **Song of the Mechanical Nightengale, 2010**
Personal
BOOK COVER * PENCIL|DIGITAL

4. **Get Off! Hairy, 2010**
Personal
BOOK * PENCIL|DIGITAL

5.–8. **Hair is Dead II–IV, 2010**
Personal
POSTER * PENCIL|DIGITAL

Jeannie Phan's work, rendered with a surrealist bent, reflects her interest in the micro-kingdom and the physiology of the human body. The pale palette of her delicate drawings, created with pencil, ink, and the computer, create a magical atmosphere of odd beauty. In between owl-hunting and fish-gazing, she enjoys spending time wolfing down sugary sweets in her home base of Toronto, Canada. Her first comic book is scheduled to be released in summer 2011.

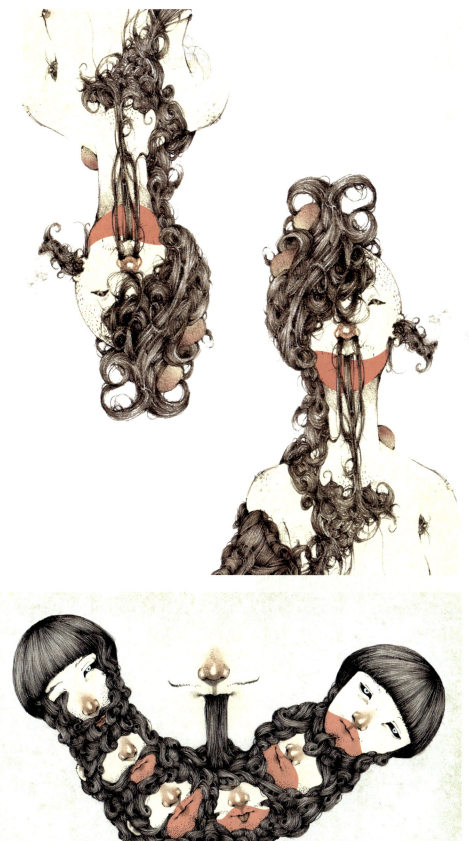

Alexey Kurbatov

Moscow-based illustrator and graphic artist Alexey Kurbatov uses watercolor and vector art to create images that have an old master's feel. Before working as an illustrator, he was a textile designer. His work can now be seen in the Russian magazine SNOB, on album covers, posters, and books.

1. **Whim, 2011**
   Personal
   POSTER * DIGITAL

2. **Fans, 2010**
   Snob Magazine
   EDITORIAL * WATER COLOR | DIGITAL

3. **Luna de Monte Carlo, 2010**
   Personal
   POSTER * WATER COLOR | DIGITAL

4. **Troubled Slumber, 2010**
   Personal
   POSTER * DIGITAL

1.___ **Artist Frida Kahlo, 2011**
Personal
POSTER * WATER COLOR | DIGITAL

2._____**General**
Charles de Gaulle, 2010
Snob Magazine
EDITORIAL * WATER COLOR | DIGITAL

3.___ **Writer Boris Strugatsky,**
2010
Snob Magazine
EDITORIAL * WATER COLOR | DIGITAL

4.____ **Actor Clint Eastwood,**
2011
Personal
POSTER * WATER COLOR | DIGITAL

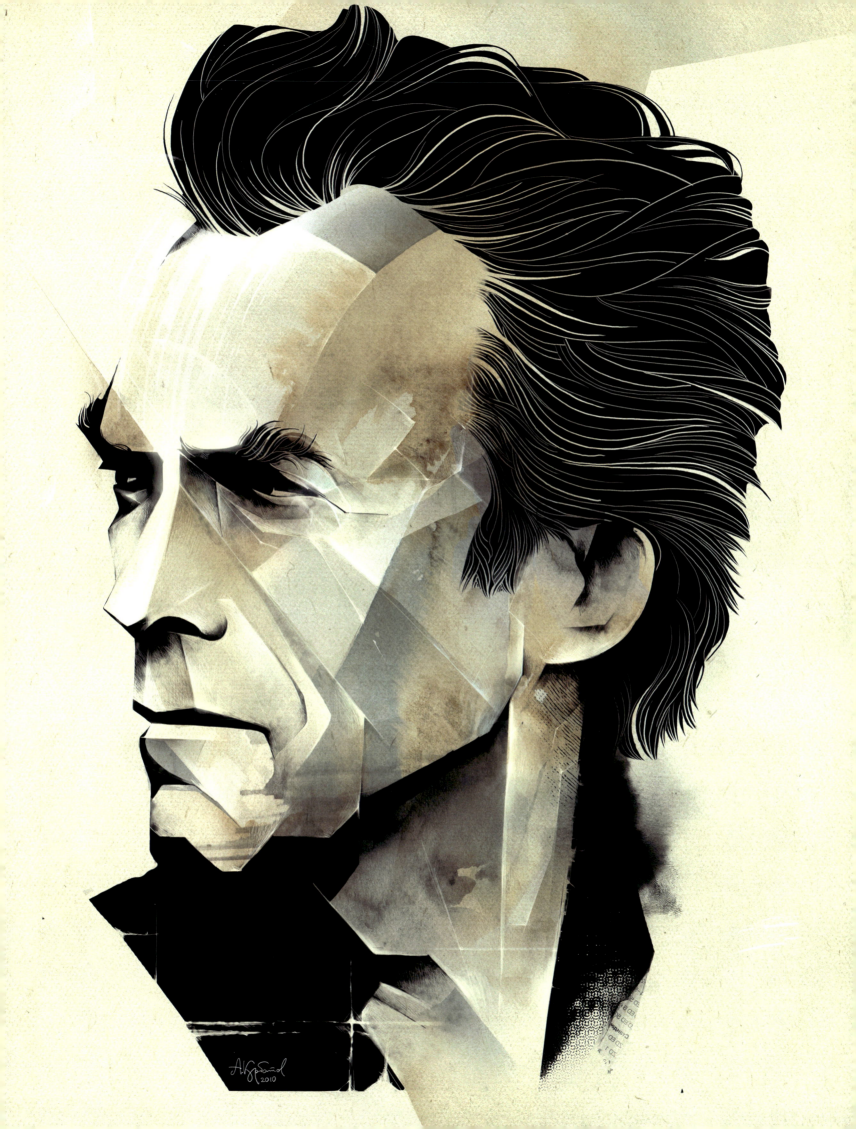

The Red Dress

The Red Dress is the London-based illustration studio of Olivia Chancellor and Ollie Bland, a husband and wife team who met while studying graphic design and illustration. Their love of illustrated vintage posters and pulp fiction inspired them to join forces to create The Red Dress, whose long client list includes the GUARDIAN, Vodafone, GQ, and POPULAR SCIENCE.

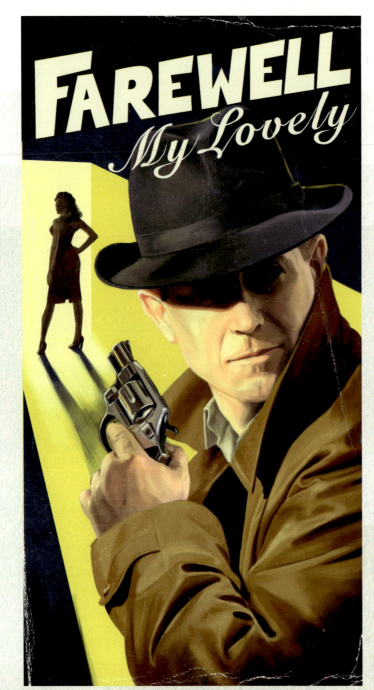

1. **Farewell My Lovely, 2011**
   Radio Times
   EDITORIAL * DIGITAL

2. **To the Manor Bourne, 2010**
   The Guardian: The Guide
   EDITORIAL * DIGITAL

3. **Bangkok Haunt, 2010**
   Bangkok Haunt
   ART DIRECTOR: STEPHANE MEGECAZE/ID3
   WEB BANNER, POSTER * DIGITAL

4. **Blood Money, 2010**
   Continuum Books
   ART DIRECTOR: ELEANOR ROSE
   BOOK COVER * DIGITAL

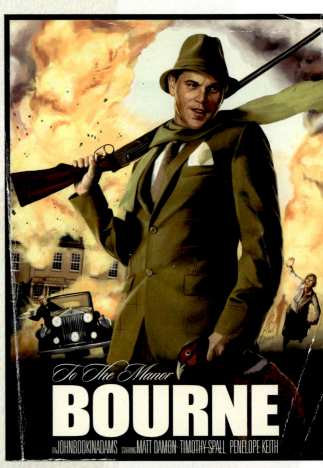

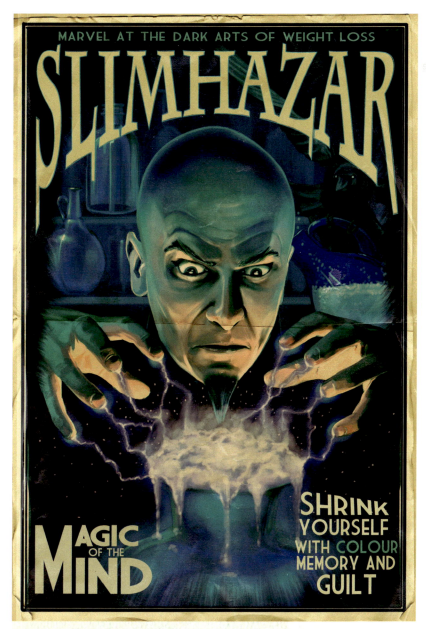

Matthew J. Laznicka

Matthew Laznicka began his illustration career creating vividly colorful creatures to delight and astound his parents. After graduating from art school, his primary goal was to saturate the world in the absurd, and boldly illustrate the insane. His inspiration comes from the work of master film directors Alfred Hitchcock and Frank Capra as well as B-grade science fiction flicks.

1. **Karma, 2010**
Black Gate Publications
PAGE * DIGITAL

2. **Lauren, 2009**
Jeff Buck
COMMISSIONED, POSTER * DIGITAL

3. **Attack of the 11 Foot Mars Woman, 2006**
Personal
POSTER * DIGITAL

4. **Sisters, 2008**
Personal
POSTER * DIGITAL

5. **Dark Horizon, 2007**
Personal
POSTER * DIGITAL

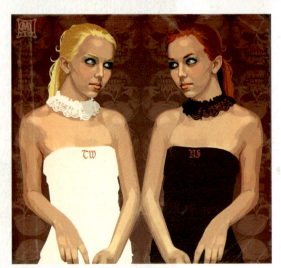

Vincent Bakkum

Vincent Bakkum was born in Holland but has called Finland home for the past two decades.

His illustrations, which deal with femininity, fashion, fruit, flowers, and birds, have been used in editorials, packaging, and advertising. Various international publications have featured his work such as ITELLA, Penguin Books, and the SUNDAY TIMES.

1. **Miss Twiggy, 2010**
   Personal
   PAINTING * ACRYLIC

2. **Orlon, 2010**
   Personal
   PAINTING * ACRYLIC

3. **Colombe, 2010**
   Personal
   PAINTING * ACRYLIC

4. **A. Dührer, 2010**
   Personal
   PAINTING * ACRYLIC

5. **Camisole, 2010**
   Personal
   PAINTING * ACRYLIC

Karen Klassen

Karen Klassen's Calgary-based studio practice produces award-winning illustrations that have been used in advertising, editorials, annual reports, fashion, and publishing. Her work uses textiles, painting, and ink to create collages that combine abstraction and realism with a nod towards fashion.

1.   **Poppy Crown, 2009**
Market Mall
CREATIVE DIRECTOR:
DAN KING / ZERO GRAVITY INC.
POSTER AD * ACRYLIC | OIL PAINTS

2.   **Detail of Bankers Hall**
Illustration, 2011
Bankers Hall
CREATIVE DIRECTOR:
RICK THOMAS / JUICE CREATIVE INC.
ADVERTISING * ACRYLIC | DIGITAL

3.   **Pink Mohawk, 2008**
Personal
EXHIBITION PIECE * ACRYLIC

4.   **Kiss, 2009**
Centrum Properties Chicago
CREATIVE DIRECTOR:
DAVID FREJ / OTHERWISE INC.
LARGE SCALE BANNERS *
ACRYLIC | OIL PAINT | DIGITAL

5.   **Butterflies, 2009**
Market Mall
CREATIVE DIRECTOR:
DAN KING / ZERO GRAVITY INC.
POSTER AD * ACRYLIC | OIL PAINTS

Chris Keegan

British illustrator Chris Keegan lives and works in London, where he creates colorful digital photomontages for a wide range of newspapers and magazines including the FINANCIAL TIMES, TIME, the OBSERVER, and THE GUARDIAN. His cover illustration for London's DESIGN WEEK magazine was chosen one of the best covers of the past 20 years. Music, design, science, architecture, and nature all provide the inspiration for his work.

1. **Firetrap Building, 2008**
Firetrap
COMMISSIONED BY STEVE ATKINSON
POSTER * DIGITAL MONTAGE

2. **Splahes, 2011**
Promotional
POSTER * DIGITAL|INK

3. **Lady, 2006**
American Publishing
BOOK COVER * PHOTO-MONTAGE

4. **World Spin Pink, 2011**
Personal
POSTER * SCREEN PRINT

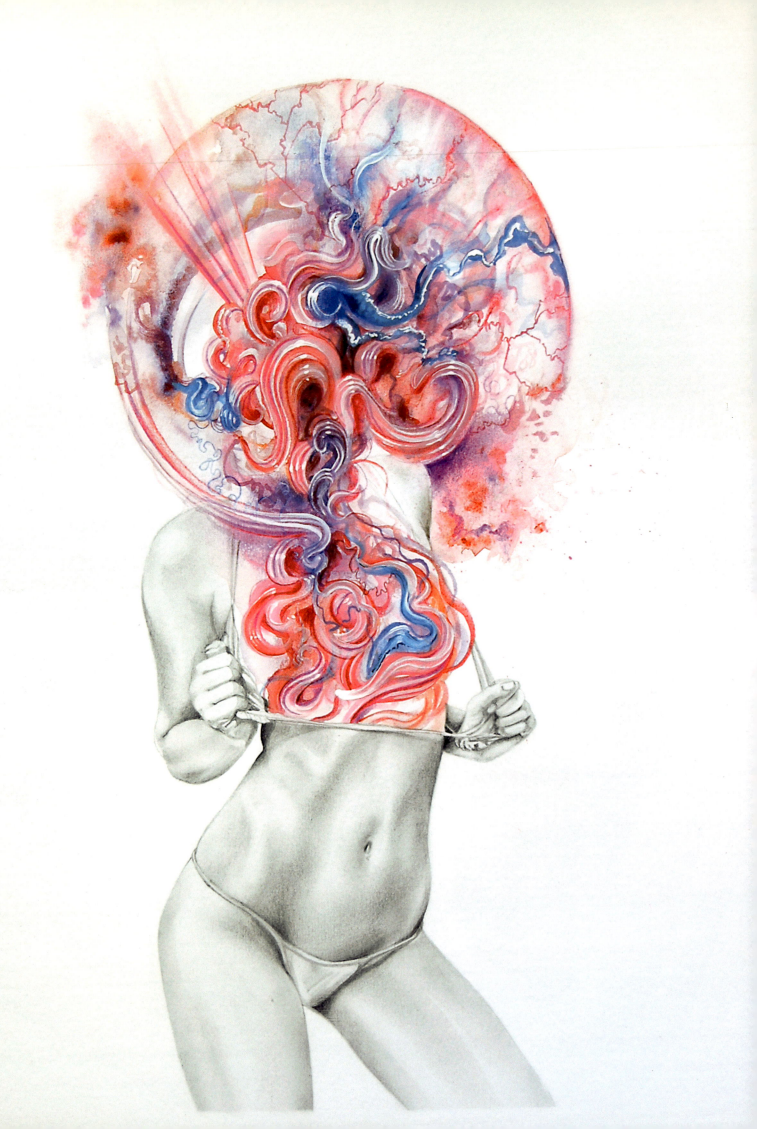

James Roper

The hyper-colorful and detailed work of James Roper reflects his influences, which range from the Baroque to anime. His process involves collecting untold amounts of images from the internet and then collaging them in Photoshop to create a working guide. Painting from this guide, he changes things along the way if need be, ultimately creating his distinct and dynamic dynamic paintings. A wide variety of publications have featured his images, including DAZED AND CONFUSED, PAPERCRAFT 2, and COMPUTER ARTS. Galleries in London, New York, and Barcelona have exhibited his work. He lives and works in Manchester, UK.

Bryony Lloyd

Bryony Lloyd assembles illustrative collages from her home studio in London, UK. Her work, influenced by all things surreal with nostalgic nods to the 1960s and 1970s, mixes acrylic paint, ink, collage, and printmaking techniques with digital manipulation in Digital. These retro images with a contemporary twist have been used as editorial illustrations for WIRED magazine and in Selfridges's THE SHOE PAPER.

1. **Wink, 2011**
It's Nice That
COLLAGE. * PAINT | PRINT | COLLAGE

2. **Josephine, 2011**
Urban Outfitters
POSTER * ACRYLIC PAINT | INK | COLLAGE.

3. **Virgo, 2010**
Selfridges
EDITORIAL * COLLAGE | DIGITAL

4. **Nymph, 2011**
It's Nice That
COLLAGE. * PAINT | PRINT | COLLAGE

5. **Serge & Jane, 2011**
Personal
INK | COLLAGE | DIGITAL.

Michael Gillette

Music has always been the main inspiration for illustrator Michael Gillette. It brought him to London during the rise of Britpop to collaborate with artists such as St. Etienne and Elastica, and to San Francisco in 2001, where he worked for Beck, the Beastie Boys, Levis, Nokia, and Greenpeace. He counts Edmund Dulac, Peter Blake, Bob Peak, David Hockney, and Ingres as just some of the influences on his work. Over the years, he has fallen in and out of love with various techniques, working with acrylics, the computer, and watercolors, always keeping an open mind to new ways of working.

It is the city of San Francisco, where he continues to live and work, that continues to inspire his work.

There he takes photographs, is working on a retrospective book of his work, and is considering making children's books and animated shows.

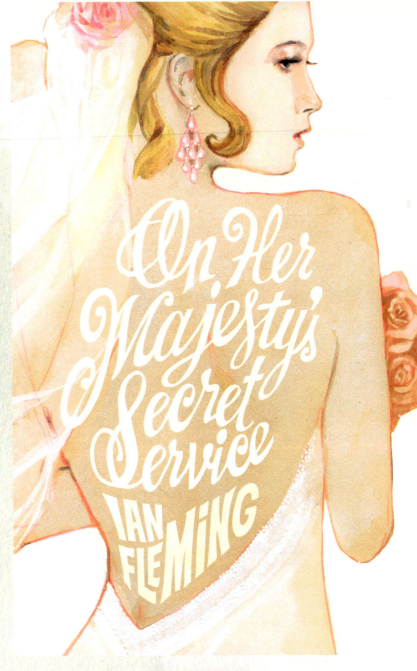

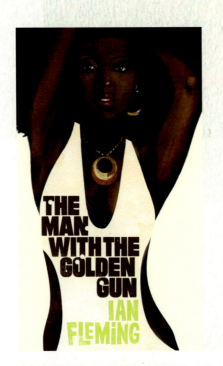

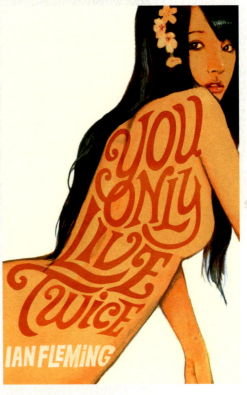

Michael Latimer

The style of UK-based artist Michael Latimer fluctuates between painting, doodling, and drawing on canvas, wood panels, and paper. It is the music he's listening to, which could be anything from Slayer to folk music, that most influences the mood and tone of his pieces. Recent projects include a series of graphics for Enjin Skateboards and a line of prints and T-shirts at his own Lowercase Industries.

1   **Striking Distance, 2011**
Personal
ART PRINT * HAND DRAWN | PAINT | DIGITAL

2   **Craters, 2011**
Personal
ART PRINT * HAND DRAWN | PAINT | DIGITAL

3   **Fall Over, Spring Back, 2011**
Personal
ART PRINT * HAND DRAWN | PAINT | DIGITAL

4   **1969, 2011**
Personal
ART PRINT * HAND DRAWN | PAINT | DIGITAL

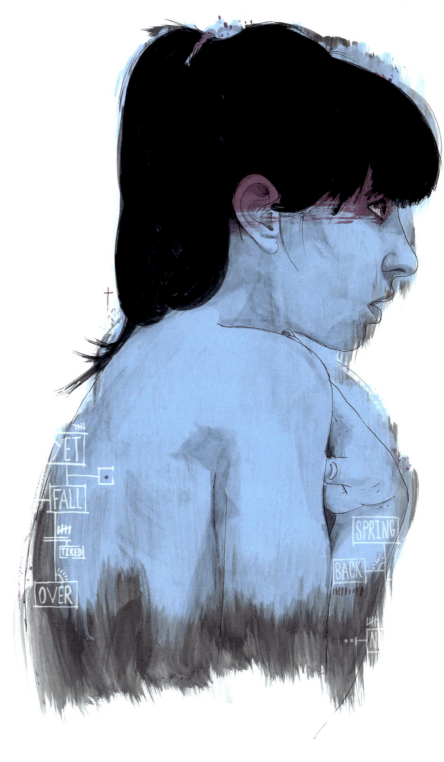

Illustrators Unlimited
The Essence of Contemporary Illustration

Edited by Robert Klanten, Hendrik Hellige

Interviews and preface by James Gaddy

Artist biographies by Rebecca Silus

Cover by Hendrik Hellige for Gestalten

Cover illustration by Irana Douer

Layout by Hendrik Hellige for Gestalten

Typeface: Nautinger by Moritz Esser, Treza by Benjamin Gomez

Foundry: www.gestaltenfonts.com

Project management by Julian Sorge and Vanessa Diehl for Gestalten

Production management by Martin Bretschneider for Gestalten

Proofreading by Leina Gonzalez

Printed by Offsetdruckerei Grammlich, Pliezhausen

Made in Germany

Published by Gestalten, Berlin 2011

ISBN 978-3-89955-371-0

BIBLIOGRAPHIC INFORMATION PUBLISHED BY THE DEUTSCHE NATIONALBIBLIOTHEK. THE DEUTSCHE NATIONALBIBLIOTHEK LISTS THIS PUBLICATION IN THE DEUTSCHE NATIONALBIBLIOGRAFIE; DETAILED BIBLIOGRAPHIC DATA ARE AVAILABLE ONLINE AT

HTTP://DNB.D-NB.DE.

NONE OF THE CONTENT IN THIS BOOK WAS PUBLISHED IN EXCHANGE FOR PAYMENT BY COMMERCIAL PARTIES OR DESIGNERS; GESTALTEN SELECTED ALL INCLUDED WORK BASED SOLELY ON ITS ARTISTIC MERIT.

THIS BOOK WAS PRINTED ACCORDING TO THE INTERNATIONALLY ACCEPTED ISO 14001 STANDARDS FOR ENVIRONMENTAL PROTECTION, WHICH SPECIFY REQUIRE-MENTS FOR AN ENVIRONMENTAL MANAGEMENT SYSTEM. THIS BOOK WAS PRINTED ON PAPER CERTIFIED BY THE FSC®.

GESTALTEN IS A CLIMATE-NEUTRAL COMPANY. WE COLLABORATE WITH THE NON-PROFIT CARBON OFFSET PROVIDER MYCLIMATE (WWW.MYCLIMATE.ORG) TO NEUTRALIZE THE COMPANY'S CARBON FOOTPRINT PRODUCED THROUGH OUR WORLDWIDE BUSINESS ACTIVITIES BY INVESTING IN PROJECTS THAT REDUCE CO_2 EMISSIONS (WWW.GESTALTEN.COM/MYCLIMATE).